Interests and Behaviours of Real Estate Market Actors in Commercial Property

T0330606

This book is a theory-led conceptual account of the Principal-Agent problem and related concepts of Behavioral Real Estate economics, a decade after the real estate crisis of 2008. Data from 52 qualitative interviews undertaken with appraisers, real estate brokers, and property owners is used to argue that the reality is more nuanced and influenced by the interests of different real estate market actors. The book provides a sketch of the relationship dynamics between real estate investors and service providers in the markets of Austria and Central and Eastern Europe.

While investors manage real estate portfolios and have to deal with particular legal systems, regulations, and norms, they often appoint service providers who have a comprehensive understanding of the local context. This work aims to highlight that this relationship between the real estate market actors creates an information asymmetry that may constitute the basis of conflicts of interest as well as Principal-Agent problems. Furthermore, the work underlines that the services provided by appraisers and real estate brokers to investors may strongly influence the profit the investor can generate from a transaction. It could be therefore inferred that the investor inclines towards a certain type of result from a service provider over the others. The present research has revealed that investors are guided by certain interests and undertake to steer the service providers in a favored direction. This book is essential reading for anyone interested in the nuances of Behavioral Economics and real estate.

Dr Alina Nichiforeanu is Senior Manager in the Transaction Real Estate division of Ernst & Young Austria. She holds a Doctorate in commercial real estate valuation from the Vienna University of Economics and Business. She also attended further programs in real estate management at Harvard Business School. She is a member of the Royal Institute of Chartered Surveyors. Dr Alina Nichiforeanu has over 16 years of experience in the Austrian and Central and Eastern European (CEE) real estate markets, assessing local business environments, acting as a bridge between companies' headquarters and subsidiaries, and leading intercultural teams. She has a proven track record of successfully concluded transactions, optimizing and repositioning distressed commercial real estate assets, as well as construction and leasing projects, with a robust global network. Her areas of expertise are asset and portfolio management, transactions and M&A's, property management, as well as corporate real estate, gathered at multinational companies in Austria and the CEE region.

Interests and Behaviours of Real Estate Market Actors in Commercial Property Valuation

Alina Nichiforeanu

Routledge
Taylor & Francis Group
LONDON AND NEW YORK

First published 2021
by Routledge
2 Park Square, Milton Park, Abingdon, Oxon OX14 4RN

and by Routledge
52 Vanderbilt Avenue, New York, NY 10017

Routledge is an imprint of the Taylor & Francis Group, an informa business

British Library Cataloguing-in-Publication Data
A catalogue record for this book is available from the British Library

Library of Congress Cataloging-in-Publication Data
Names: Nichiforeanu, Alina, author.
Title: Interests and behaviours of real estate market actors in commercial property valuation / Alina Nichiforeanu.
Description: Abingdon, Oxon ; New York, NY : Routledge, 2020. | Includes bibliographical references and index.
Identifiers: LCCN 2020008589 (print) | LCCN 2020008590 (ebook) | ISBN 9780367482473 (hardback) | ISBN 9781003038801 (ebook)
Subjects: LCSH: Real estate investment—Psychological aspects. | Commercial real estate—Valuation.
Classification: LCC HD1382.5 .N527 2020 (print) | LCC HD1382.5 (ebook) | DDC 333.33/872—dc23
LC record available at https://lccn.loc.gov/2020008589
LC ebook record available at https://lccn.loc.gov/2020008590

ISBN: 978-0-367-48247-3 (hbk)
ISBN: 978-0-367-51759-5 (pbk)
ISBN: 978-1-003-03880-1 (ebk)

Typeset in Goudy
by Apex CoVantage, LLC

Contents

Acknowledgments

I wish to thank all my interview partners, who took their time and shared from their experiences as experts, decision-makers, and advisors in the fields of transactions and valuation of commercial real estate. Needless to mention that they are absolved of any responsibility for the conclusions I have reached.

I am indebted to my entire real estate network for providing a confidential and trustworthy basis and for helping me contribute to the academic literature on commercial real estate, in the fields of Behavioral Real Estate economics and Principal-Agent theory related to real estate valuation for transaction purposes.

Abstract

This work is a theory-led conceptual account of the Principal-Agent problem and related concepts of Behavioral Real Estate economics, a decade after the real estate crisis of 2008. I use the data from 52 qualitative interviews undertaken with appraisers, real estate brokers, and property owners to argue that the reality is more nuanced and influenced by the interests of different real estate market actors. I also aim to provide a sketch of the relationship dynamics between real estate investors and service providers in the markets of Austria and Central and Eastern Europe. Here, I underline the interrelation between these two groups of actors on two levels: theoretically and empirically.

I focus on the theoretical level to analyze the context in which the two groups operate and their performed role in a real estate transaction to highlight the interplay between real estate investors and service providers active in various countries. While the investors manage real estate portfolios and deal with different legal systems, regulations, and norms, they often appoint service providers who have a comprehensive understanding of the local context.

Overall, this study aims to highlight that this relationship between the real estate market actors creates an information asymmetry that may constitute the basis of conflicts of interest as well as Principal-Agent problems. Furthermore, the paper underlines that the services provided by appraisers and real estate brokers to investors may strongly influence the profit the investor can generate from a transaction. Therefore, it could be inferred that the investor inclines towards a certain type of result from a service provider over the others. The present research has revealed that investors are guided by certain interests and undertake to steer the service providers in a favored direction.

The study addresses the theoretical polarization between Principal-Agent theory and Behavioral Real Estate, in which empirical data were collected and analyzed to infer the hypotheses about specific types of actions and behavioral strategies of the two groups of market actors. These hypotheses form the basis of the empirical analysis, investigated with the qualitative program called NVivo. The results of the interviews provide evidence for a Principal-Agent relationship between investors and service providers, supporting the hypothesis that the investors as well as service providers are aware of the conflict of interests and try to steer the process.

The topic of valuation has been gaining relevance for investors in the past years, showing the current developments and their accompanying risks, such as local real estate bubbles, which have turned valuation into a field relevant for analysis. The appraiser follows concretely defined requests according to the valuation standards in use. However, the ideal of the objective appraiser does not match the reality of market actors with diverging interests.

Over the past decade there has been a significant increase in the real estate academic literature and research, mostly in areas such as investment, property valuation and appraisal, real estate finance, environmental affairs, as well as Behavioral Economics or Behavioral Real Estate.

The findings of Behavioral Real Estate show that appraisers have a certain leeway in their decisions, and that this leeway can be subject to potential influences. This study challenges the notion of the objective appraiser and analyzes the leeway subject to external influences of market actors for transaction-based valuations and mandatory valuations to establish commercial value.

Building up on this structure, the problem definition of this work includes various aspects of behavioral research in real estate valuation as well as Principal-Agent problem evidence.

Acronyms and terminology

Advisor	Service provider; real estate broker and/or appraiser
AI	Appraisal Institute
AIREA	American Institute of Real Estate Appraisers
ANEVAR	The Romanian Authorized Appraisers Association
Asset	Real estate property
Asset class	Logistics, office, retail real estate properties
Appraiser (USA) or Valuer (UK)	Certified expert in property valuation
ARE	Association of Real Estate Experts
BREEAM	Building Research Establishment Environmental Assessment Methodology
Broker	Person mandated to act as an intermediary for the sale or purchase of commercial real estate in exchange for a commission
BVFI	German Federal Association for the Real Estate Industry
Cap rate	Capitalization rate
CARI	Collegium Academic Rerum Immobilium
Company size	Small, <50 employees; medium, 50–249 employees; large, >250 employees
CEE	Central and Eastern Europe; in this study, limited to Czech Republic, Hungary, Slovakia, Slovenia, and Romania
Client	Contracting party; principal; representative of a real estate company which manages, develops, and/or invests in commercial real estate property
CRE	Counsellors of Real Estate
DGNB	Deutsche Gesellschaft für Nachhaltiges Bauen (German Sustainable Building Council)

EVS	European Valuation Standards
Development	Commercial real estate property in the process of construction
FIABCI	Fédération Internationale des Administrateurs de Biens Conseils Immobiliers
FRICS	Fellow of the Royal Institute of Charted Surveyors
IAS	International Accounting Standards
IFRS	International Financial Reporting Standards
IMMQU	Association for the Promotion of Quality in the Real Estate Industry
IVS	International Valuation Standards
IVSC	International Valuation Standards Council
LBG	Liegenschaftsbewertungsgesetzt (Austrian Valuation Law)
Membership	Enrollment in at least one real estate association
MRICS	Member of the Royal Institute of Charted Surveyors
ÖGNI	Österreichische Gesellschaft für Nachhaltige Immobilienwirtschaft (Austrian Association for Sustainable Real Estate)
ÖNORM	Austrian Norm
ÖVI	The Austrian Association of the Real Estate Industry
Region	Austria, Czech Republic, Hungary, Slovakia, Slovenia, Romania
RICS	Royal Institute of Charted Surveyors
SIOR	Society of Industrial and Office Realtors
Standing investment	Already-developed real estate property, which brings a regular income through an active management
SVP	Standards of Valuation Practice
TEGoVA	The European Group of Valuers' Association
Transaction	Sale-purchase agreement for at least one commercial real estate property or portfolio
Organization	Real estate organization or association
QDA	Qualitative data analysis
ULI	Urban Land Institute
USPAP	Uniform Standards of Professional Appraisal Practice

Figures

Annexes

1 Introduction

1.1. Relevance of the topic

Real estate is a "multifaceted economic good" that is differentiated from other economic goods and whose properties are being examined by various economic disciplines (Bone-Winkel et al. 2016: 22). Real Estate Economics as a discipline of economic sciences is distinct in nature from other branches of economics and transcends the scope of momentary observations of reality, in that its findings serve as a source of knowledge for better management strategies for market actors. Research efforts in the field aim to "support real decisional processes through theoretical decision-making approaches and to bring forth solutions for improvement" (Bone-Winkel et al. 2016: 47–48).

The significance of the real estate sector has often been underestimated by politicians and society alike, despite its effects on the entire economy. "The industry has been growing on average by 2% yearly since 2008" (Bone-Winkel et al. 2016: 42) and the attractiveness of investing in real estate has strongly risen since the recession. Nearly all institutional investors such as investment funds, credit institutes, insurance companies, or public organizations have invested at some point in real estate assets.

The concept of real estate valuation plays a particularly significant role in the real estate investment field. Investing in real estate requires a careful and transparent assessment process to ensure that the long-term capital commitment takes place under conditions of risk minimization or profit maximization, respectively, and to confer legitimacy upon the investment decision.

That is why ethics remains an ever-relevant aspect of real estate business and, implicitly, real estate valuation, to provide a transparent portrayal of the interests and goals of all parties involved without limiting them.

The focus on transparency and ethics is crucial in the construction and real estate sector to promote sustainable development, as well as avoid unfair advantages, corruption, and aggressive business practices of opportunistic hedge funds.

Maring (2015) regards the valuation of real estate as an ethical challenge, requiring a symbiosis between philosophy and economics on a normative, ethical level. "This is found in the normative and ethical foundations of real estate quality valuation, which are expanded by including social and ecological aspects, as well as by defining recommendations for appraisers from an ethical, normative perspective" (Maring 2015: 237).

Properties are often evaluated differently depending on each party's point of view. Owners' internal assessments will likely estimate a higher value, since their personal interests influence their perception. The buyers, on the other hand, rather focus on the labor they need to invest in the property and assess its value on a much lower level due to careful price considerations.

At the same time, an investor has a certain pressure to (re)invest, which supports the formation of real estate bubbles. New leases can have different effects on cash-flows and valuations. The financing bank employs a cautious value approach (such as the lending value in Germany) to minimize the risk. It could also lead to the abuse of information benefits, with the more informed side using these advantages in an opportunistic manner and trying to influence the valuation outcome.

When individuals or business partners do not have the same level of information, asymmetric information between the parties involved might be the result. Such a case can be described as "moral hazard." The concept is already used in the standard economic discourse and could also become an integral part of the property valuation process. Measures aimed at increasing revenue can send false signals and lead to detrimental consequences, such as setting the wrong incentives for the decision-maker.

Moral hazard is defined as "the post-contractual opportunism between transaction partners, in which one party has limited information about the behavior of the other" (Gabler Wirtschaftslexikon 2017). This can occur in the real estate valuation process if there are information asymmetries between the parties involved, where one has less information than the other.

An example would be the withholding of any information which would increase the property's value. The buyer could have the information that an investment by a third party will take place near the property, or that there will be a change in the zoning – both scenarios leading to an increase in the value of the property in question.

Another important characteristic is the assumption of the Principal and the Agent being asymmetrically informed. For instance, it is often problematic for the appraiser (Agent) to have to work in the interest of the investor (Principal), especially in cases where the latter has concrete expectations about the value of the property, which he expects the appraiser to confirm. This "mutual" valuation agreement is oftentimes a prerequisite for future collaboration.

This topic of asymmetric information on the real estate markets becomes even more complex when real estate agents who pursue their own interests or those of the client are included into the analysis.

A problematic case, for instance, would be when a broker is hired and estimates a higher initial price just because he wants to receive the mandate for the transaction. Later, the Agent tries to "push down" the purchase price, since the initial estimated price is not an accurate reflection of the market value. The "Agent" (real estate broker) usually possesses a knowledge advantage (information asymmetry) that can be used in different ways either for the benefit or to the detriment of the "Principal" (investor).

Building upon the agency theory (to be comprehensively presented in the next chapter), James Graaskamp – an established researcher in real estate appraisal in the 1970s–1980s – contributed significantly to the field of real estate. His reflections on property valuation and investment analysis were grounded in Behavioral Economics and Behavioral Real Estate. It is important to "first understand the behavior and motivation of market agents, in order to then assess the feasibility of the project" (Robbins & Ahearn 1994: 150).

James A. Graaskamp regards the property valuation process as a systematic application of Behavioral Economics and research "in which the appraiser strives to fit the attributes of the subject property into a market context driven by decisions of market actors" (Robbins & Ahearn 1994: 149).

Kinnard et al. (1997) further discuss the "pressure exerted by clients" within the framework of Behavioral Real Estate, while Wolverton und Gallimore (1999) provide scientific insights into the importance of *client feedback* on real estate valuation.

An investigation into the respective interests, motivations and actions of both advisors/brokers and decision-makers on the market is essential to increase transparency and shed light on relevant issues in the valuation process of commercial property. This book also challenges the concept of the objective real estate appraiser.

The possibilities of influencing valuation decisions are analyzed in this book using qualitative research in the form of personal interviews. Furthermore, the scope of action for the market actors, as well as the decisional bandwidths for property appraisers, are presented and linked to the theory of Behavioral Real Estate and information asymmetries.

Finally, Salzman and Zwinkels (2017: 77) point out that "although it is commonly known that the real estate markets are rather liquid, the majority of academics assume that these markets are efficient; it is assumed that participants act in accordance with rationality." This study challenges the rationality of the market actors, trying to highlight their specific interests in real estate transactions or valuation processes.

1.2. Design of the interviews and theories behind

Greiner (2008: 384) stresses that "behaviorally oriented research in real estate valuation is directly relevant for practice." Furthermore, "Behavioral Real Estate allows procedures to be structured more transparently and opens the way for improvement suggestions. It thus makes sense to approach property valuation process and real estate investment from a behavioral perspective" (Greiner 2008: 389).

From these issues and arguments, the following questions are derived in the study:

- How can we concretely illustrate the interests of market actors with respect to the type of property and the real estate cycle in the appraisal process?
- Are there any information asymmetries between market actors? If yes, what is their nature and how can they be classified?
- Is the concept of "moral hazard" relevant for the commercial property appraisal process? How can it be defined in this case?

The aim is to find concrete answers to these questions by means of presenting theoretical and institutional approaches to real estate valuation, considering asset classes and market actors within the framework of real estate economics. Building up on existing literature, we take note of the following assumptions for this study:

- Focus will be on two categories of market actors: service providers (real estate brokers and advisors for commercial real estate, including appraisers) and clients (real estate project developers and investors).
- The interviewed market actors reside in the following countries: Austria and Central Eastern Europe (limited to countries with high Austrian investment rates: Romania, Slovakia, the Czech Republic, Hungary, and Slovenia).
- The scope of the analysis will be limited to appraisals related to transactions (buying and selling of real estate).
- The type of real estate analyzed is limited to commercial real estate properties, with a focus on retail, office, and logistics real estate properties.

This work differentiates between market actors in the real estate industry – investors and project developers acting as buyers or sellers, as well as appraisers and brokers representing the client or contractor – and the interests depending on the asset class in the commercial real estate sector.

Harmonized standards are necessary for the *business ethics* aspects of the trade, sale, and valuation of commercial real estate, irrespective of the object in question is a retail property, an office, or a logistics property.

Concepts such as "Principal-Agent problem" and "moral hazard" as rationale of information asymmetries in the real estate appraisal process will be comprehensively discussed in the next chapters. Furthermore, international real estate organizations, as well as ethics standards and codes of conduct will be presented.

Even though there is no specific ethical law to solve the Principal-Agent problem, real estate organizations draw up rather strict, international ethical rules that act as guidelines and/or requirements for their members.

To answer the aforementioned questions, I will consider the theories of information asymmetries, as well as Behavioral Real Estate approaches, legislative, and institutional aspects of real estate appraisals and transactions and results from existing research.

The study can be classified in the following phases:

Phase 1. A detailed literature review including a survey on real estate literature on commercial real estate and real estate appraisal process, as well as the related literature in disciplines such as Behavioral Economics and Principal-Agent theory.
Phase 2. Two focus groups were identified (clients and advisors), and a total of 52 in-depth qualitative interviews were run to gather the opinions of market leaders, experts, and advisors in the real estate industry. Austria and the CEE markets were selected with the scope of providing diversity among the behavior and interests of the specific market actors.
Phase 3. An attempt to link the academic literature on real estate economics with the qualitative data gathered from the interviewed market actors to provide a perspective for the discussion on Behavioral Real Estate as a special field of Behavioral Economics. By explaining the background of Evolutionary Economics and Behavioral Economics, the present discussions on the interests of the market actors when valuating commercial real estate properties for transaction purposes might become easier to understand.

The basis of this work is a combination of literature research on Behavioral Real Estate economics as well as agency theory to explain the Principal-Agent problem in real estate appraisal for transaction purposes. There is overlapping literature on Behavioral Economics, but the focus of this transdisciplinary analysis always remains on the fact that market actors behave differently in different contexts and are aware of the conflict of interests that arise.

By studying the background of Behavioral Real Estate, the present discussions on the interests of the market actors when valuating commercial real estate might become easier to understand and to take a position on.

The question on the market actors' interests when assessing a property can be also put in a normative way: *How can we describe and understand the reasoning behind the valuation practice in the years to come?*

Bibliography

Bone-Winkel, Stephan et al. (2016): *Teil A Einführung in die Immobilienökonomie*. 1. Begriff und Besonderheiten der Immobilie als Wirtschaftsgut. 2. Bedeutung der Immobilienwirtschaft. 3. Immobilienökonomie als wissenschaftliche Disziplin, in Schulte, Karl-Werner et al. (eds.) *Immobilienökonomie I. Betriebswirtschaftliche Grundlagen*. Band 5. Grundlegend überarbeitete Auflage. Berlin and Boston: de Gruyter

Gabler Wirtschaftslexikon, Springer Fachmedien Wiesbaden (2017): www.springer-gabler.de (last accessed 27.01.2020)

Greiner, Martin (2008): Kapitel 4.1.3. Verhaltenstheorie: Behavioral Real Estate, in Schulte, Karl-Werner (ed.) *Immobilienökonomie*. Band IV. Volkswirtschaftliche Grundlagen. München: Oldenbourg

Kinnard, William N. et al. (1997): Client Pressure in the Commercial Appraisal Industry: How Prevalent Is It? *Journal of Property Valuation and Investment*. Vol. 15. No. 3

Maring, Matthias (2015): *Vom Praktisch-Werden der Ethik in interdisziplinärer Sicht: Ansätze und Beispiele der Institutionalisierung, Konkretisierung und Implementierung der Ethik*. Band 7. Karlsruhe: KIT Scientific Publishing

Österreichische Gesellschaft für Nachhaltige Immobilienwirtschaft (ÖGNI) (2017): www.ogni.at/ (last accessed 27.01.2020)

Robbins, Michael L. & Ahearn, Sean C. (1994): Section II. Appraisal, Feasibility, and Special Use Analysis. Chapter 5. The Price of Wilderness and Scenic Beauty: A Methodology for the Inventory and Appraisal of Wilderness and Scenic Land, in DeLisle, James R. & Sa-Aadu, Jay (eds.) *Appraisal, Market Analysis, and Public Policy in Real Estate. Essays in Honor of James A. Graaskamp*. American Real Estate Society. Real Estate Research Issues. Vol. 1. Boston: Kluwer Academic Publishers

Salzman, Diego & Zwinkels, Remco (2017): Behavioral Real Estate. *Journal of Real Estate Literature*. Vol. 25. No. 1

Wolverton, Marvin L. & Gallimore, Paul (1999): Client Feedback and the Role of the Appraiser. *Journal of Real Estate Research*. Vol. 18. No. 3

2 Information asymmetries, Behavioral Real Estate, ethics, and valuation

2.1. Information asymmetries

2.1.1. Market actors in commercial real estate

The following chapter illustrates the theoretical background as related to market actors in the real estate industry. First, the respective players in the real estate market are defined and then divided into two main categories: on one side, the contracting party, such as real estate investors, real estate developers, real estate joint stock companies, real estate funds, etc.; and on the other hand, the contractors: providers of real estate services, such as real estate brokers and appraisers.

Schulte et al. (2008: 3) split the real estate market participants into different actors from the construction, real estate, and finance industries according to the institutional aspects of the real estate economy: "real estate investors, real estate project developers, real estate service providers such as brokers and appraisers, tenants, real estate financial institutions and construction companies." The first three categories will be the focus of this study.

A division between client and contractor is made with the aim of investigating and documenting the unequal distribution of information between these categories.

Real estate investors, such as financing bodies or contractors, are defined primarily according to the "purpose of the investment" (Teufelsdorfer 2015: 6) and are divided into private and institutional investors (Gondring & Lammel 2001: 251; Bone-Winkel et al. 2016: 26).

The most important groups of institutional investors whose interests and strategies make up the focus of this analysis consist of (Gondring & Lammel 2001: 251, 266; Teufelsdorfer 2015: 6–7; Bone-Winkel et al. 2016: 26–27; Schulte et al. 2016: 141):

- Capital management companies and special funds that have a long-term investment strategy with net asset value raising as their goal.
- Insurances and pension funds, which may invest a small part of their capital in real estate and have a risk averse investment strategy.

- Real estate leasing companies that concern themselves with medium- to long-term rental of land, buildings, and other fixed assets.
- Real estate stock corporations, which show a higher risk preference and are often involved in project development.
- Foreign investors and opportunity funds that employ foreign capital to purchase, restructure, and subsequently resell high-risk securities.
- Real Estate Investment Trusts (REITs), like open real estate funds.

An additional category besides real estate investors who take over the ownership function are the real estate project developers. They are "responsible for the conception and realization of new construction projects, the revitalization of stock properties and occasionally act as a service provider of individual services for different market actors within the framework of the real estate development process" (Bone-Winkel et al. 2016: 26).

The real estate service providers are mainly appraisers; technical, legal, or financial advisors (very often employed for the course of a transaction, but also for management or restructuring purposes); planners and project controllers during project development; or companies that provide real estate marketing and research services, facility/property management, or corporate real estate services (Gondring & Lammel 2001: 253–254; Bone-Winkel et al. 2016: 27; Schulte et al. 2016: 158–167).

External service providers essentially consist of "real estate brokers, who are employed in departments such as rentals and sales within large and internationally active brokerage companies" (Viering et al. 2007: 103). Falk et al. (2004: 573) give the following definition for the real estate agent: "A broker provides remunerated intermediation services for the conclusion of contracts or the opportunity to conclude contracts." Furthermore, "the real estate broker has information duties towards his client with respect to conclusions of business transactions, legal notices or the granting of taxation information" (Viering et al. 2007: 111). Although "brokers can counsel their client as to the sales value of the object, they are entitled in this respect to a certain *assessment leeway* in that they act as a knowledge provider but owe the client neither investigations nor specific inquiries" (Viering et al. 2007: 111).

Brokers and appraisers active in Austria and Central Eastern Europe constitute the focus of this work. I examine the extent and type of information asymmetries that can arise in the assessment and valuation of commercial properties between service providers on the one side and real estate investors and developers on the other, as well as the ways to prevent these asymmetries.

2.1.2. Principal-Agent theory

Jensen and Meckling (1976) were among the first to describe the Principal-Agent theory (also called Agency Theory). The name is derived from the concept of the "Principal-Agent problem." According to this theory, information asymmetries arise during a contractual relationship between the client (Principal) and the contractor (Agent). "The Agent enjoys a certain degree of decisional freedom and the ability to conduct business for the Principal. These actions can in turn bring an advantage to the Principal, due to the information advantage the Agent has" (Jensen & Meckling 1976: 5).

"Information asymmetry normally arises within exclusivity contracts wherein one party (the Agent) limits the ability of the Principal to enter other contractual relationships with other Agents" (Bisin & Guaitoli 1998: Non-technical Summary).

> Nevertheless, such a contract can be designed in such a way that the Agent can withdraw at any time; in such a case, the Principal must provide optimal incentives and create an attractive contract so that the Agent no longer takes external alternatives into consideration.
>
> (Englmaier et al. 2010: 27)

Göbel (2002: 99) presents the example of the "lessor and the tenant as a Principal-Agent relationship in the real estate market" and identifies "the handling of the rented property, as well as the rent payment, as sources of potential conflicts" (Göbel 2002: 99).

This study will examine the relationship between institutional investors, property owners and developers (Principals), and real estate consultants, real estate brokers, and appraisers (Agents), as well as the ways in which their interests and actions relate to the property valuation process described in the following chapter.

Agency theory assumes an unequal distribution of information – "the less information is available about the motives, interests and the actions of the Agent, the higher the risk that he pursues his own interests to the detriment of the Principal" (Saam 2002: 6).

> The information problem arises for the Principal because he cannot observe the actions of the Agent; a further issue is that of risk distribution between Principal and Agent, since both have an incentive to pursue different actions due to their different interests.
>
> (Saam 2002: 8)

The Principal-Agent problem is further compared with the transaction costs theory[1] ("performance and exchange relationships between members of structured societies" [Dietl 1993: 108]): in this case, "imperfect information is another form of limited rationality, with knowledge gaps present in both cases" (Dietl 1993: 134).

In the literature, asymmetric information is often broken down into several types: hidden characteristics, hidden action, and hidden information (Alparslan 2006: 21–24; Dietl 1993: 137–144; Laffont & Martimort 2002: 3). Göbel (2002: 103) and Saam (2002: 29) also add hidden intentions as a further category. "The risk of *hidden characteristics* (latent features) arises before the contract signing and describes the quality uncertainty from the Principal's side" (Saam 2002: 29).

The Agent can hide information about his qualifications or goods or services offered prior to the commencement of a performance (ex-ante) from the Principal. Therein lies the risk for the Principal of selecting an inadequate contractual partner, an effect known in the literature as *adverse selection* (Dietl 1993: 138; Göbel 2002: 101).

Hidden information, however, arises after the conclusion of the contract when the Agent can choose to share his knowledge or experience opportunistically. "He can take advantage of his knowledge on insider information, influence, already occurred events or prospects of success" (Saam 2002: 29).

Hidden intentions as a "risk of the asymmetric information scenario before the conclusion of the contract are a sub-category of *hidden characteristics*, such as when the Agent displays different behavioral characteristics such as honesty or transparency in order to accomplish his interests" (Göbel 2002: 103).

Hidden action arises after concluding the contract. In such cases, agency issues arise, such as "consumption on the job, when the Agent privately takes advantage of the Principal's resources, or shirking, the intentional concealment of the true performance potential" (Göbel 2002: 102). Furthermore, it is frequently impossible for the Principal to be aware of the correlation between the Agent's actions and the result, since "exogenous factors can [also] influence the outcome or the performance" (Alparslan 2002: 23).

Moral hazard is an agency problem that is defined in slightly diverging ways in the literature. Saam (2002), Dietl (1993), Bisin and Guaitoli (1998), and Laffont and Martimort (2009) describe the concept as a classic case of *hidden action*. Göbel (2002), however, conflates hidden action and hidden information as concurring causes of moral hazard.

A general explanation of the potential risk of asymmetric information in property valuation or appraisal can be described as follows:

> By the mere fact of delegation, the Principal often loses any ability to control those actions that are no longer observable, either by the Principal who offers the contract or by the court of law that enforces it.
>
> (Laffont & Martimort 2002: 145)

The types of information asymmetries in Principal-Agent relationships and their suggested solutions are summarized in the Figure 2.1.

This work aims to further investigate information asymmetry problems that arise in the context of real estate valuations and affect and/or influence Agents (real estate brokers and appraisers) and Principals (real estate investors and developers).

Further evidence on information asymmetries between Principals and Agents, as well as concerning licensing the appraisers, has been given by Corgel and Jaffe (1984), Colwell and Trefzger (1992), Leland (1979), and Shapiro (1986), who note that low-quality appraisers would be produced if the Principals cannot differentiate between the quality of the valuation reports; thus, adverse selection means that the quality of the appraisers differ and there is even moral hazard

Time	*Types*	*Problems*	*Problem causes*	*Solutions and instruments*
Ex-ante	Hidden characteristics	Adverse selection	The Agent displays false characteristics	Harmonization of interests: guarantees, collateral, reputation
Ex-ante Ex-post	Hidden intentions	Adverse selection Hold-up	The Principal is dependent on the Agent	Harmonization of interests: redemption clauses, acceptance guarantees, counter-transactions
Ex-post	Hidden action	Shirking Consumption on the job	Cost of monitoring, monitoring capability, resource elasticity	Harmonization of interests: profit participation, sanctioning possibilities, monitoring, reporting
Ex-post	Hidden information	Fringe benefits	Self-serving decisions of the Agent	Signaling, screening, self-selection via balance sheet, quality accreditations, monitoring, reporting

Figure 2.1 Asymmetric information (Göbel 2002: 100, 110; Dietl 1993: 144, 153)

involved "where the initial quality of agents is the same" (Shapiro 1986). This problem can be solved if the agents establish similar reputations, such as licenses, professional designations, courses, and tests.

In a next chapter, the most relevant international real estate organizations will be presented, together with their efforts to bring forth policy suggestions for the aforementioned challenges and issues. The fundamental point of similarity between the real estate organizations presented lies in their stance on integrity and transparency as a means to combat information asymmetries.

2.2. Behavioral Real Estate

The neoclassical behavioral model has notably been used in business and economics in order to explain the actions of economic agents. Nevertheless, neoclassical models offer an incomplete depiction of reality. For instance, it has been argued and proven that decision-makers cannot fully take into account all potential consequences.

It is for these reasons that behavioral approaches were developed, "as a reaction to these demonstrations of market inefficiency and the awareness of the influence of human behavior and social contagion" (Salzman & Zwinkels 2017: 79), but also "from the need to include such circumstances into the theoretical framework of the model" (Greiner 2008: 374).

As Greiner (2008: 374) further notes, "explaining and designing the decisional processes of real estate market actors make up the core task of real estate economics, whereby the focus lies on researching the behavior of real estate market actors, especially that of the appraisers." This approach is known as Behavioral Real Estate, and within this branch of Real Estate Economics, valuation has encountered the most research attention so far.

In the mid-1970s, Graaskamp (1977: 8) introduced a paradigm as an attempt to understand the market actors in commercial property:

> Economics is behavioral science, descriptive of the economic behavior of people under various conditions. It is the appraiser's task to predict how people, both buyers and sellers, will behave with respect to the subject property when it is exposed for sale. People make values and determine prices.

Diaz (2002) was among the first scientists to describe properties in terms of maximum productivity ("highest and best use") and to analyze the extent to which the property's potential to generate earnings is being exploited. The "highest and best use can deviate from the original use and even influence the valuation result" (Greiner 2008: 374).

Further investigations into the behavior of real estate appraisers include the behavioral pattern of expert appraisers for real estate transactions ("Selection of comparison transactions," Diaz 1990b), in which they choose between three to six comparable transactions, but also the finding of Gallimore and Wolverton (1997) that the appraiser is influenced if he knows the selling price of a property to be valued.

These two insights are used by Greiner (2008: 382) to note that "people run the risk of accepting qualitatively inferior results if they increase cognitive efficiency while at the same time reducing cognitive effort."

Further behavioral insights relevant for the real estate appraiser are the *availability bias* (attention is disproportionately focused on the last information considered) (Gallimore 1994, 1996) and the *validation bias* (seeking out positive information about a property to confirm the assessment result), or the *anchoring effect* or *appraisal smoothing* (Diaz & Wolverton 1998) – taking past assessment values into account as *anchors* for future assessments if the appraisers rate a property more than once. According to the findings of Diaz and Hansz (1997), appraisers rely on previous value judgments if they are not familiar with a particular market.

Furthermore, Kinnard et al. (1997) have shown in a study how the pressure exercised by clients influences an evaluation and thus, the appraisers. Furthermore, "client's feedback plays a crucial role in the confirmation of the estimated buying price" (Greiner 2008: 383).

Levy and Schuck (1999) too have found in a study on experts from New Zealand that experienced clients exert influence and pressure on appraisers by emphasizing the positive aspects of a property and concealing negative characteristics as much as possible.

James A. Graaskamp contributed to the topic of ethics in real estate valuation. According to his theories, the interests of small investors and communities are insufficiently taken into account. He believed in the importance of including social aspects in real estate business and emphasized that the rights of private and public owners are inextricably linked together.

James A. Graaskamp undertook significant behavioral research in real estate valuation in the 1970s and 1980s. His mentor and forerunner in the field was Ratcliff, whose approaches to Behavioral Economics and Behavioral Real Estate enabled Graaskamp to justify decisions that appear irrational at first sight.

Since most collateral losses hurt communities and small investors, Graaskamp began working on a more comprehensive approach to feasibility analysis and valuation. His book, *Guide to Feasibility Analysis*, is still considered the norm. Graaskamp was first and foremost a real estate appraiser, a fact confirmed by DeLisle (2004: 17) and connected to Behavioral Real Estate:

> Unlike many of his contemporaries, he [Graaskamp] recognized that appraisal was a behavioral art that focused inherently on stochastic market artifacts. Furthermore, he noted that prices are set through negotiations between buyers and sellers and that to predict the outcome of these negotiations one had to first define the most probable buyers for those real estate rights. Once likely buyers were identified, the analyst could reconstruct the logic that would determine the buyer's and seller's subjective valuations.

One of the most significant contributions of Graaskamp to the topic of real estate valuation was the definition of a new concept, *most-probable selling price*, as a valuation artifact. The operationalization of this concept is given by behavioral methods in the course of property valuation.

Graaskamp managed to justify seemingly irrational decisions through Behavioral Real Estate. Even if decisions do not appear to be rational in the economic sense, they could still be justified from the perspective of the decision-makers. He provided two explanations in that regard: on the one hand the short-term perspective and thinking of market actors, and on the other, the need to first understand the rationale behind the decision.

He believed that "researchers should employ behavioral approaches to understand the value drivers of decision makers on the real estate market, which models they employ and what backgrounds they have" (DeLisle 2004: 5–6).

In addition, "behavior-oriented research in real estate valuation helps less experienced appraisers gain information about the efficient but perhaps subconscious actions of experienced appraisers, while expert appraisers may become aware of systematic errors in their behavior" (Greiner 2008: 384). Last, but not least, research results in Behavioral Real Estate can be embedded in ethical standards for real estate valuation (Diaz 2002; Greiner 2008).

Investigating the interests and behaviors of local and international real estate market actors can also deepen the understanding of the current socioeconomic and real estate business environment. The observed actions of real estate market actors during the valuation process can be used in governance research to develop the appropriate incentives or regulations such that the Principal acts in the interest of the Agent.

2.3. Current ethics standards and codes of conduct

"In order to indicate credibility and gain trust in a specific performance-based relationship, signaling costs are incurred in the form of memberships, warranties, business reports or quality assessments" (Dietl 1993: 136). Real estate market actors such as brokers, advisors or appraisers purchase memberships in nationally and internationally recognized associations, so as to raise their credibility.

Gondring and Lammel (2001: 1144) provide a detailed definition of associations:

> Associations are organizations that arise from the voluntary cooperation of natural and legal persons. They have an inner division of labor, a statute, as well as binding, longer-term objectives (usually in the form of programs), on the basis of which they seek to impose the interests of their members against the state and other interest groups.

The real estate industry deals extensively with issues of an ethical nature. National and international real estate associations and organizations are working on solutions and creating different codes of conduct to improve transparency and optimize business relationships.

The international real estate market endeavors at all times to increase transparency and support communication and cooperation between shareholders. It is for this reason that codes of conduct have been created by various professional real estate organizations on an international level. The member states of such organizations implement the codes of conduct at a national level, according to their specific legislation and best practices.

In recent years, the most important industry players from more than 50 countries have developed an industry-wide code of conduct; to this end, all areas of the real estate industry were mapped to improve ethical foundations. Thus, the largest association worldwide was officially established in October 2014, on the occasion of a meeting at the United Nations in New York, with the aim to develop and implement the first industry-wide ethical standards for the real estate industry. The *International Ethics Standards Coalition (IESC)* consists of 106 leading professional associations, organizations, and real estate service providers from Asia, Europe, Oceania, and North and South America (as of January 2017).

Although many member organizations of IESC already have their own code of conduct, the new international standards should provide a common ethical foundation based on trustworthiness, integrity, and respect for real estate market participants. The introduction of transparent ethical standards should improve services in the real estate sector and enhance procedural transparency in business.

The *American Appraisal Institute (AI)* is an international association of real estate appraisers that was created in the year 1991 after the merger between the *American Institute of Real Estate Appraisers* (AIREA, founded in the year 1932) and the *Society of Real Estate Appraisers* (founded in the year 1935).

The AI has a rigid code of conduct and standards for internationally active appraisers; as with *RICS (Royal Institute of Charted Surveyors)*, failure to comply with the rules of the code leads to disciplinary action. The ethics principles of the Appraisal Institute contain rules concerning behavior towards the public, for the maintenance of an appropriate professional status, and for supporting the association. In addition, the appraiser is expected to provide sufficient analyses, opinions, and conclusions and observe confidentiality (Appraisal Institute 2017: Ethics and standards).

The *Counsellors of Real Estate (CRE)* are an exclusive organization founded in 1953 that consists of 1,100 (Counsellors of Real Estate 2017) real estate consultants and executives worldwide that are entitled to display the CRE label in their name (similar to the MRICS or FRICS title). Although the organization does not have a formal code of conduct, it wants to demonstrate through their rigorous application process that all members have a high level of real estate competence and comply with the core ethical values of the organization (integrity, competence, community, trust, selflessness) (Counsellors of Real Estate 2017: Ethics & Standards).

FIABCI (Fédération Internationale des Administrateurs de Biens Conseils Immobiliers) (FIABCI 2017), also known as "International Real Estate Federation," is an association founded in 1949 and is a worldwide network of real estate professions that supports cooperation in the field of commercial real estate and enables worldwide business relations. It is one of the most representative organizations of the real estate industry worldwide and has a consultative status in the Economic and Social Council (ECOSOC, Economic and Social Council) of the United Nations.

ULI (Urban Land Institute) is another international real estate organization headquartered in Washington, D.C. and founded in December 1936. The ULI Code of Ethics consists of ten guiding principles dealing with the topic *respect (acceptance)*, being strongly linked to sustainability and to the responsible development and use of resources (environment). In general, it is also stressed that the customer and the public should always be respected, also with regard to future generations (ULI 2017: Code of Ethics).

A real estate association which engages extensively in ethical and professional standards is *RICS – Royal Institute of Charted Surveyors*. The British association of real estate professionals was founded in 1868 and was awarded the Royal Charter of the United Kingdom by Queen Victoria in 1881. The RICS code of conduct applies worldwide to all members – MRICS (Member of the Royal Institute of Chartered Surveyors) and FRICS (Fellow of the Royal Institute of Chartered

Surveyors). It consists of obligations relating to the business activities in the real estate sector, agreements with regard to conflicts of interest and transparency, promotion of training measures, and arrangements for compulsory liability insurance.

The efforts of real estate organizations show how challenging it is to have global institutionalization of ethical norms and to create appropriate rules of conduct. The cornerstones of ethics and morality are theoretical concepts usually encountered and taught in educational contexts.

For ethical business, however, they are necessary instruments aiming to create transparency for the real estate industry. These consist of compliance standards (corporate governance, corporate social responsibility) of large companies, ethics certifications by independent real estate associations, and the respective standards and codes of conduct of real estate organizations.

To summarize, we can take note of the following universally valid ethical foundations and principles that relate to real estate business practice, especially with respect to appraisals, counseling, and brokerage:

- Confidentiality and non-disclosure of information to third parties.
- Sharing of all relevant information between contractual partners.
- Integrity, transparency, and respect towards all parties involved.
- Respecting national laws and norms.
- Responsibility towards business partners.
- Expertise and worthy representation of the real estate business, as well as constant professional development to remain up-to-date with the latest knowledge in the field.

2.4. Commercial property valuation

2.4.1. Short note on commercial real estate

Schulte et al. (2008: 2) regard real estate economics as a still young scientific field, whose goal is to "support decisional processes of real estate market actors and contribute to their improvement via solution proposals," thus explaining and shaping them. By resorting to a simplified approach to real estate characteristics, the following four categories arise (Schulte et al. 2008: 3): "commercial, residential, industrial and special real estate properties." "Real estate properties are durable goods that . . . are available for use throughout decades or centuries" and are defined by the property (land) on which they are based (Heymann 2000: 25). They take on the character of a secondary investment if they merely provide the framework for business activities and are not directly linked to generate immediate returns (Ropeter 1998: 67–68).

The main attributes of real estate as a tangible investment are defined by Bone-Winkel (1994: 23): space units that "are available for a limited period of time" and "are offered on the market throughout the service life of the

1	Office and service-oriented properties	Office buildings, business centers, hotels, restaurants
2	Retail properties	Shopping centers, self-service markets, department stores, specialist market centers, inner-city sales areas
3	Industry and logistics properties	Logistics real estate such as warehouses, industrial parks, factory buildings, other production facilities, technology parks
4	Multi-functional real estate	Medical practices, offices, and apartments in a building
5	Special properties	Leisure properties, seniors' facilities
6	Special properties/non-profit organizations	Buildings belonging to ecclesiastical or charitable institutions

Figure 2.2 Types of commercial properties by type of use (Ropeter 1998: 71–73; Platz 1993: 28; Arens 2016: 85; Bone-Winkel 1994: 33)

object," for which the owner receives a "certain price for the contractual use of the object."

Commercial real estate has a multitude of different uses, which can be structured in the following categories, according to literature, as shown above:

In this study, the focus is on examining the interests of market actors in the assessment and valuation of office, retail, and logistics real estate.

Investment in real estate takes place in different forms and the factors to consider range beyond economic aspects to legal, technical, and financial considerations. In summary, four categories of criteria are relevant for an investment decision (Ropeter 1998: 74–80), namely: location (micro and macro), development (architecture, costs, timeline, quality, and political and public frameworks), tenancy (contract design, vacancy, and indexation) and commercialization possibility (third-party use, loss of earnings, and disposal options).

According to Platz (1993: 107–108), real estate management today is no longer only *function preserving* and regards the property as a passive investment, but rather as an *actively cared for production factor*. Maintenance, as well as contract management or rental and ancillary cost accounting (Platz 1993: 104, 107), remain necessary, "but property management is also expected to operate dynamically and maximize yields" (Platz 1993: 108).

In the following part, the appraisal methods for the aforementioned real estate classes will be presented. The appraisal process can take place at every development stage of the project: for plots that have not been built on yet, but have a construction authorization and a zoning plan; for existing buildings as part of a project in development, where the previously developed and/or rented property is sold in so-called forward purchase deals; or for completed buildings that are to be used by the final investor as a classical investment or for its own use.

2.4.2. *Real estate valuation and appraisal methods*

Often the term real estate appraisal relates to the task of the real estate broker to provide a rough estimation of the possible price of a property.

> As the real estate market has lower transparency and the offered products are rather heterogeneous, the real estate market actors (investors, in particular buyers and sellers of real estate, but also investors that only use their property) rely on appraisers to anticipate the possible value of the selling price.
>
> (Bienert 2009: 38)

Falk (1992: 403) emphasizes the complexity of property valuation, especially in the case of commercial real estate assets and explains that "there should be three main judgements before starting the valuation process: consideration on the asset type, on the past changes and the exact criteria to be examined in the case of each valued property."

The valuation of commercial real estate is a central point of real estate management and takes place on numerous occasions (Leopoldsberger et al. 2016: 427) such as when "buying or selling, financing, auctioning of real estate, or for expropriations, division of property, company takeovers, performance measurements, information purposes, insurance certifications or tax reasons."

A real estate assessment (valuation, appraisal) is necessary either to obtain information or to comply with regulations.

The reasons for a property valuation can also be divided into two categories, depending on the main focus of the activity (WKÖ & Kranewitter 2011):

- From the company's perspective, occasions for a valuation of real estate are, for example, sales (including merger, M&As, IPOs), the preparation of national or international financial statements, performance measurement and benchmarking (through internal measurement of market values and their development), as well as risk management for the identification of value enhancement opportunities and risks.
- From the real estate asset point of view, property valuation generally occurs during the sale process as well as for financing, investor pitching, credit examinations, etc.; in addition, a real estate valuation is necessary in the case of court value assessments for expropriation or compensation.

There are several valuation events that should lead to the same outcome independent of the valuation method or occasion:

- *Transaction purposes: purchase and sale of individual properties or portfolios, real estate rental, and sale price break down, which is purpose of this work.*
- Financing.
- Legal disputes.
- Internal controlling and/or external accounting.
- Tax bases.
- Insurance.

The property is generally viewed through the lens of its market value, from the point of view of what value it has for the owner who sells it. A real estate valuation should be carried out in an objective manner, irrespective of purpose, and yield considerations should of course be included in the analysis.

According to Feilmayr (2009), property value is teleological, so a value system is required to see how the process of comparison takes place when an asset to be appraised is compared to a reference object and "the unknown price is inferred from the known one." In philosophy, value is defined as a relationship between an object and a scale created *by an assessing person*. Here, the decision-making options relevant to the "assessing" real estate market actors are playing a significant role in the valuation process (Feilmayr 2009: 34).

Institutional investors use yield specifications[2] as parameters for property appraisal, considering the type of use and the location (Platz 1993: 87) of real estate properties.

Property valuation is a procedure governed by national and international regulations, norms, and laws and relies on the application of economic, legal, and technical knowledge and assumptions to determine a market value for real estate property investments.

Since commercial real estate is subject to the regulatory requirements of national and international companies, a market-oriented assessment requires appropriate market monitoring that is based on analyzing the respective market and location-specific value drivers. Irrespective of financing, transactional, and brokerage interests, a correct identification of market values is to be ensured.

The profitability of commercial real estate is influenced by increases in value during the hold period (when the commercial real estate assets are under management), but also by a certain interest level from the financers, by the management costs, and gross cash flow resulting from the use of the property. In addition, a cycle-optimized commercialization is facilitated by regular market and asset valuations and appraisals of the respective property.

"Full indications of market prices are rarely available, which is why valuations are needed" (Leopoldsberger et al. 2016: 427). The following sections describe the most common valuation methods, which can be split into several categories, depending on the income or property type:

- The *Comparative Value Method* is an appraisal used merely for developed and undeveloped plots of land, provided there are sufficient comparable land plots in the region, with similar characteristics.

- The *Income Approach* focuses on the economic side of a property, and is mainly used in the commercial sector for income-generating properties, such as commercial real estate, mixed-use developments, or rented residential real estate.
- The *Asset Value Method* determines the value of the property based on the buildings and outdoor and other facilities, mainly where self-use prevails.
- The Anglo-American *Discounted Cash Flow* is a further valuation alternative often used by investors, also known under the term Capital Value Method, which is not to be equated with the Income Approach.
- The *Residual Value* is used especially for real estate property in the development phase, which determines the residuum (the residual) "left for an investment if the other amounts are known or predetermined" (Platz 1993: 70).

On the international level, there are valuation standards which are not regulated by legislation or rules. The internationally active professional organization RICS (Royal Institute of Chartered Surveyors) has campaigned for an international standardization of real estate valuation and accordingly published the *RICS Valuation – Professional Standards Global*. The *Red Book* of RICS is regarded as the standard in international real estate appraisal and its methods, such as DCF (Discounted Cash-flow), Investment Method, Comparison Method, or Depreciated Replacement Cost, are also used in Austria and Central Eastern Europe, especially by international investors.

According to the *RICS Red Book*, the commercial or fair value of a property is "the value of an asset for the owner or future owner under investment considerations or with respect to operational goals." It can be determined by publicly ordered and sworn experts and/or certified valuation experts, but also by so-called internationally recognized "charted surveyors" or by independent experts with or without a completed certification.

The valuation procedures – also known as new, Anglo-Saxon, or international evaluation procedures – are often considered more appropriate to be used, with partial criticism directed at the strong leverage effect of the multipliers and the high level of detail in assumptions over a long period of time. The question of determinability arises, but also the *need to assess what interests play a role* and how much leeway is available in the context of a real estate valuation, which continues to be an ethical issue.

In practice, the DCF method is mainly used for the preparation and analysis of investment decisions. What is lacking for it to be applied as a "sole valuation procedure" is the Internal Rate of Return (analysis of interest rates derived from market transactions) and the "feeling for this particular interest rate" on behalf of the valuation expert, which has little connection to actual property interest rates (Feilmayr 2009: 55).

2.4.3. *Normative literature and standards for appraisers*

After the financial crisis of 2008 when the real estate element was probably the main cause, central banks and financial market authorities initiated a deep exploration for improving the quality of the valuation reports, which led to a collaboration between auditors (with IAS and IFRS background) and appraisers (responsible for IVS and EVS).

The first International Valuation Standard (IVS) was published in 1985 and it mostly contained standards and best practices for the valuation process itself. Its successor (IVSC) has developed additional standards and recommendations together with EVS, the European Valuation Standards.

After employing the opinions of appraisers and auditors, the IVS came to several recommendations for appraisers, the main areas being code of conduct, education, independency, client relation, transparency, and ethics.

Although the IVS, EVS, and USPAP are similar for ethical behavior and code of conduct required for appraisers, there are still compliance challenges in practice, as Van den Berg and Hordijk (2017) note:

- An appraiser is supposed to *act impartial and independent*, but it might become an issue when the appraiser works for a large, international company that is involved in many transactions.
- A distinction should be made between *valuation and valuation advice*, and the appraiser should clearly define his assignment in the valuation report.
- Non-market valuations (e.g., valuations conducted for *taxation purposes* which use the basis of Mass Appraisal methods) might be in conflict on the local level to how an appraiser must work according to the IVS.
- Confidentiality versus transparency of the information used by appraisers and made available through the valuation reports – information which might be sensitive, but valuable, for the quality of the outcome.

To conclude, the international standards and recommendations for the appraisers are rather vague and depend very much on the country's legislation. Moreover, even in Austria where the Valuation Law dates since the 1920s, there is little room allocated to describe and settle the behavior and activity of the appraisers. The law and norms leave a blank space in this regard, while concentrating on the normative, technical part of the valuation process. Furthermore, the valuation law, norms, or standards do not specify any given or accepted bandwidth.

Notes

1 The transaction cost theory has also been criticized in the literature, for instance by Ghostal und Moran (1996) who stress the dangers of such a "bad for practice" theory for corporate managers. Ghostal und Moral emphasize the sources of "organizational advantage" and argue that transaction cost theory has to be more closely related to practice.

2 "The yield gives information on the net interest rate of the capital employed, the development of which results from additional production costs and depreciation (book value)" (Platz 1993: 82). The simplified formula is: annual net income x 100/total value or total acquisition price.

Bibliography

Alparslan, Adem (2006): *Strukturalische Prinzipal-Agenten-Theorie. Eine Reformulierung der Hidden-Action Modelle aus der Perspektive des Strukturalismus.* 1. Auflage. Wiesbaden: Deutscher Universitäts-Verlag

Appraisal Institute (AI) (2017): www.appraisalinstitute.org/ (last accessed 13.01.2020)

Arens, Jenny (2016): Teil B Typologische Aspekte der Immobilienökonomie. 1. Unterscheidung nach Immobilienarten, in Schulte, Karl-Werner et al. (eds.) *Immobilienökonomie I. Betriebswirtschaftliche Grundlagen.* Band 5. *Grundlegend überarbeitete Auflage.* Berlin and Boston: de Gruyter

Austrian Association of Real Estate Experts (ARE) (2017): www.are.or.at/ (last accessed 13.01.2020)

Bach, Hansjörj & Mändle, Markus (2008): 6. Immobilienwirtschaftliches Verbandswesen. 6.1. Immobilienwirtschaft und Verbände, in Schulte, Karl-Werner et al. (eds.) *Immobilienökonomie.* Band IV. Volkswirtschaftliche Grundlagen. München: Oldenbourg

Bienert, Sven (2009): Abschnitt I. Einführung in die Immobilienbewertung. 1. Bewertungsanlässe – Überblick, in Bienert, Sven & Funk, Margret (eds.) *Immobilienbewertung Österreich.* Band 2. Auflage. Wien: ÖVI Immobilienakademie

Bisin, Alberto & Guaitoli, Danilo (1998): *Moral Hazarad and Non-Exclusive Contracts.* National Macroeconomics and Industrial Organization. Discussion Paper No. 1987. Centre for Economic Policy Research, London

Bone-Winkel, Stephan (1994): *Schriften zur Immobilienökonomie. Das strategische Management von offenen Immobilienfonds unter besonderer Berücksichtigung von Gewerbeimmobilien.* Köln: Rudolf Müller Bau-Fachinformationen

Bone-Winkel, Stephan et al. (2016): Teil A Einführung in die Immobilienökonomie. 1. Begriff und Besonderheiten der Immobilie als Wirtschaftsgut. 2. Bedeutung der Immobilienwirtschaft. 3. Immobilienökonomie als wissenschaftliche Disziplin, in Schulte, Karl-Werner et al. (eds.) *Immobilienökonomie I. Betriebswirtschaftliche Grundlagen.* Band 5. Grundlegend überarbeitete Auflage. Berlin and Boston: de Gruyter

Bundesverband für die Immobilienwirtschaft (BVFI) (2017): www.praxisverband.de/ (last accessed 13.01.2020)

CBRE: www.cbre.com/ (last accessed 13.01.2020)

Collegium Academicum Rerum Immobilium (CARI) (2017): www.cari.at/ (last accessed 13.01.2020)

Colliers: www.colliers.com/ (last accessed 13.01.2020)

Colwell, Peter & Trefzger, Joseph (1992): Impact of Regulation on Appraisal Quality. *Appraisal Journal.* Vol. 60

Corgel, Jack & Jaffe, Austin (1984): Alternative Forms of Quality Regulation in the Market for Appraisal Services. *Real Estate Appraiser Analyst.* Vol. 50

Counsellors of Real Estate (CRE) (2017): www.cre.org/ (last accessed 13.01.2020)

Cushman & Wakefield: www.cushmanwakefield.com/ (last accessed 13.01.2020)

DeLisle, James R. (2004): *Graaskamp: A Holistic Perspective.* White Paper 112. Original Draft in DeLisle, J.R. & Worzala, E. (2000): *Honor of James A. Graaskamp: Ten Years After.* PP. 51–86. Washington, DC: Runstad Center for Real Estate Studies

Diaz, Julian (1990a): How Appraisers Do Their Work: A Test of the Appraisal Process and the Development of a Descriptive Model. *Journal of Real Estate Research.* Vol. 5. No. 1

Diaz, Julian (1990b): The Process of Selecting Comparable Sales. *The Appraisal Journal.* Vol. 58. No. 4

Diaz, Julian (1997): An Investigation into the Impact of Previous Expert Value Estimates on Appraisal Judgement. *Journal of Real Estate Research*. Vol. 13. No. 1

Diaz, Julian (2002): *Behavioral Research in Appraisal and Some Perspectives on Implications for Practice*. RICS Foundation Research Review Series. August 2002: www.rics-foundation.org (last accessed 21.04.2020)

Diaz, Julian & Hansz, James A. (1997): How Valuers Use the Value Opinion of Others. *Journal of Property Valuation and Investment*. Vol. 15. No. 3

Diaz, Julian & Hansz, James A. (2001): The Use of Reference Points in Valuation Judgement. *Journal of Property Research*. Vol. 18. No. 2

Diaz, Julian & Levy, Deborah (2004): Multicultural Examination of Valuation Behavior. *Journal of Property Investment and Finance*. Vol. 22. No. 4

Diaz, Julian & Wolverton, Marvin L. (1998): A Longitudinal Examination of the Appraisal Smoothing Process. *Real Estate Economics*. Vol. 26. No. 2

Dietl, Helmut (1993): *Institutionen und Zeit. Die Einheit der Gesellschaftswissenschaften*. Band 79. Tübingen: Mohr Siebeck

Englmaier, Florian et al. (2010): *Optimal Incentive Contracts Under Moral Hazard When the Agent Is Free to Leave*. Industrial Organization. Discussion Paper No. 7914. Centre for Economic Policy Research, London

European Group of Valuers Associations (TEGoVA): www.tegova.org/ (last accessed 13.01.2020)

European Group of Valuers Associations (TEGoVA) (2009): *European Valuation Standards (EVS)*. 6. Auflage

European Group of Valuers Associations (TEGoVA) (2016a): *Europäische Bewertungsstandards*. 8. Auflage

European Group of Valuers Associations (TEGoVA) (2016b): *European Valuation Standards*. Auflage

Falk, Bernd (1992): *Gewerbe-Immobilien*. Band 5. Überarbeitete Auflage. Landsberg and Lech: Verlag Moderne Industrie

Falk, Bernd et al. (2004): *Fachlexicon Immobilienwirtschaft*. 3. Aktualisierte und erweiterte Auflage. Köln: Immobilien Informationsverlag Rudolf Müller

Fédération Internationale des Administrateurs de Biens Conseils Immobiliers (FIABCI) (2017): www.fiabci.org/ (last accessed 13.01.2020)

Feilmayr, Wolfgang (2009): *Grundstücksmärkte und Immobilienbewertung, Fachbereich Stadt- und Regionalforschung*. Wien: Technische Universität

Gallimore, Paul (1994): Aspects of Information Processing in Valuation Judgement and Choice. *Journal of Property Research*. Vol. 11. No. 2

Gallimore, Paul (1996): Confirmation Bias in the Valuation Process: A Test for Corroborating Evidence. *Journal of Property Research*. Vol. 13. No. 4

Gallimore, Paul et al. (2000): Decision-Making in Small Property Companies. *Journal of Property Research*. Vol. 18. No. 6

Gallimore, Paul & Wolverton, Marvin L. (1997): Price-Knowledge-Induced Bias: A Cross-Cultural Comparison. *Journal of Property Valuation and Investment*. Vol. 15. No. 3

Gerlach, Heinz et al. (1994): *Die Gewerbeimmobilie als Kapitalanlage*. 4. Aktualisierte und erweiterte Auflage. Freiburg: Rudolf Haufe

Ghostal, Sumantra & Moran, Peter (1996): Bad for Practice: A Critique of the Transaction Cost Theory. *The Academy of Management Review*, Vol. 21, No. 1

Göbel, Elisabeth (2002): *Neue Institutionenökonomik. Konzeption und betriebswirtschaftliche Anwendungen*. Stuttgart: Lucius & Lucius

Gondring, Hanspeter & Lammel, Eckhard (2001): *Handbuch Immobilienwirtschaft*. 1. Auflage. Wiesbaden: Betriebswirtschaftlicher Verlag Gabler

Graaskamp, James A. (1972): A Rational Approach to Feasibility Analysis. *The Appraisal Journal*, in Stephen, P. J. (1991): *Graaskamp on Real Estate*. Washington, DC: Urban Land Institute

Graaskamp, James A. (1977): *The Appraisal of 25 N. Pinckney: A Demonstration Case for Contemporary Appraisal Methods*. Madison, WI: Landmark Research

Graaskamp, James A. (1982): A *Guide to Feasibility Analysis: Update, Excerpts from Unpublished Revision*, reprinted in Stephen, P. Jarchow (1991): *Graaskamp on Real Estate*. Washington, DC: ULI-the Urban Land Institute

Greiner, Martin (2008): Kapitel 4.1.3. Verhaltenstheorie: Behavioral Real Estate, in Schulte, Karl-Werner (ed.) *Immobilienökonomie*. Band IV. Volkswirtschaftliche Grundlagen. München: Oldenbourg

Harvard, Tim (2001a): Valuation Reliability and Valuer Behavior. *RICS Research Paper*. Vol. 4. No. 1

Harvard, Tim (2001b): An Experimental Evaluation of the Effect of Data Presentation on Heuristic Bias in Commercial Valuation. *Journal of Property Research*. Vol. 18. No. 1

Hauptverband der allgemein beeideten und gerichtlich zertifizierten Gerichtssachverständigen (2017): www.gerichts-sv.at/ (last accessed 13.01.2020)

Heymann, Ilke (2000): *Die Entwicklung des gewerblichen Immobilienmarktes in den neuen Bunderländern. Reihe V. Volks- und Betriebswirtschaft*. Band 2521. Frankfurt am Main: Peter Lang Europäischer Verlag

IMMQU Verein zur Förderung der Qualität in der Immobilienwirtschaft (2017): www.immqu.at/ (last accessed 13.01.2020)

International Council of Shopping Centers (1994): *Shopping Center Management*. ICSC Catalog No. 173. New York: International Council of Shopping Centers

International Ethics Standards Coalition (IESC) (2017): https://ies-coalition.org/ (last accessed 13.01.2020)

International Valuation Standards (IVS) (2007): *IVSC*. 8. Auflage

International Valuation Standards Committee (IVSC) (2017): www.ivsc.org/ (last accessed 13.01.2020)

Jaffe, Austin & Corgel, Jack (1984): Should Real Estate Appraisers Be Licensed? *Real Estate Appraiser Analyst*. Vol. 50

Jensen, Michael & Meckling, William (1976): Theory of the Firm: Managerial Behavior, Agency Costs and Ownership Structure. *Journal of Financial Economics*. Vol. 3. Harvard Business School, Boston

Jones Lang Lasalle (JLL) (2017): www.jll.com (last accessed 13.01.2020)

Kinnard, William N. et al. (1997): Client Pressure in the Commercial Appraisal Industry: How Prevalent Is It? *Journal of Property Valuation and Investment*. Vol. 15. No. 3

Laffont, Jean-Jacques & Martimort, David (2002): *The Theory of Incentives: The Principal-Agent Model*. Princeton, NJ: Princeton University Press

LBG (2015): *Liegenschaftsbewertungsgesetz und bewertungsbezogene Regelungen in AußStrG und EO mit erläuternden Anmerkungen und Rechtsprechung*. Band 2. Neu bearbeitete und erweiterte Auflage. Sonderausgabe Nr. 78. Wien: Manzsche Verlags- und Universitätsbuchhandlung

Leland, Hayne (1979): Quacks, Lemons, and Licensing: A Theory of Minimum Quality Standards. *Journal of Political Economy*, Vol. 87, No. 6

Leopoldsberger, Gerrit et al. (2016): Teil E Funktionsspezifische Aspekte des Immobilienmanagements. 2. Immobilienbewertung, in Schulte, Karl-Werner et al. (eds.)

Immobilienökonomie I. Betriebswirtschaftliche Grundlagen. Band 5. Grundlegend überarbeitete Auflage. Berlin and Boston: de Gruyter

Levy, Deborah & Schuck, Edward (1999): The Influence of Clients on Valuations. *Journal of Property Investment and Finance*. Vol. 17. No. 4

ÖNORM B 1802 (1997): *Liegenschaftsbewertung*. Grundlagen. Auch Normengruppe B1

ÖNORM B 1802-2 (2008): *Liegenschaftsbewertung*. Teil 2: Discounted-Cash-Flow-Verfahren (DCF-Verfahren)

ÖNORM B 1802-3 (2013): *Liegenschaftsbewertung*. Teil 3: Residualwertverfahren

Österreichischer Verband der Immobilienwirtschaft (ÖVI) (2017): www.ovi.at/de/verband/index.php (last accessed 13.01.2020)

Österreichisches Norminstitut: ÖNORM B 1802 (2002): *Liegenschaftsbewertung Grundlagen*. Wien

Platz, Jürgen (1993): *Immobilien-Management. Prüfkriterien zu Lage, Substanz, Rendite*. 3. Auflage. Wiesbaden: Betriebswirtschaftlicher Verlag Gabler

Ropeter, Sven-Eric (1998): *Investitionsanalyse für Gewerbeimmobilien*. Köln: Rudolf Müller

Royal Institution of Chartered Surveyors (RICS) (2008): *Appraisal and Valuation Standards – Red Book*. 6. Auflage

Royal Institution of Chartered Surveyors (RICS) (2014): *RICS Valuation – Red Book/White Book: Professional Standards Global*. www.rics.org/Global/RICS_Valuation_Professional_Standards_global_2014_June2015reprint_2014edition_PGguidance_2015.pdf (last accessed 10.04.2017)

Royal Institution of Chartered Surveyors (RICS) (2017): www.rics.org (last accessed 19.04.2017)

Saam, Nicole J. (2002): *Prinzipale, Agenten und Macht. Die Einheit der Gesellschaftswissenschaften*. Band 126. Tübingen: Mohr Siebeck

Salzman, Diego & Zwinkels, Remco (2017): Behavioral Real Estate. *Journal of Real Estate Literature*. Vol. 25. No. 1

Schiller, Jürgen (2009): Abschnitt I. Einführung in die Immobilienbewertung. 6. Der Sachverständige im österreichischen Recht, in Bienert, Sven & Funk, Margret (eds.) *Immobilienbewertung Österreich*. 2. Auflage. Wien: ÖVI Immobilienakademie

Schulte, Karl-Werner & Kolb, Christian (2008): 1. Einführung in die Immobilienökonomie. 1.5. Ethik für Immobilienberufe, in Schulte, Karl-Werner et al. (eds.) *Immobilienökonomie*. Band IV. Volkswirtschaftliche Grundlagen. München: Oldenbourg

Schulte, Karl-Werner et al. (2008): *Immobilienökonomie*. Band IV. Volkswirtschaftliche Grundlagen. 1. Volkswirtschaftslehre und Immobilienökonomie. 1.1. Einführung. München: Oldenbourg Wissenschaftsverlag GmbH

Schulte, Karl-Werner et al. (2016): *Immobilienökonomie I. Betriebswirtschaftliche Grundlagen*. Band 5. Grundlegend überarbeitete Auflage. Teil C: Institutionelle Aspekte der Imobilienökonomie. Berlin and Boston: de Gruyter

Shapiro, Carl (1986): Investment, Moral Hazard, and Occupational Licensing. *Review of Economic Studies*. Vol. 53, No. 5

Stephen, P. Jarchow (1991): *Graaskamp on Real Estate*. Washington, DC: ULI-the Urban Land Institute

Teufelsdorfer, Herwig (2015): *Handbuch Immobilientransaktionen. Auswahl. Due Dilligence. Übernahme ins Portfolio*. Band 2. Aktualisierte Auflage. Wien: Linde

Urban Land Institute (ULI) (2017): http://uli.org/ (last accessed 13.01.2020)

Van den Berg, Sake & Hordijk, Aart C. (2017): *Compliance with International Valuation Standards: What Does It Mean?* Practice Paper: The Case of Netherlands, ERES eres2017_257, European Real Estate Society (ERES). https://ideas.repec.org/p/arz/wpaper/eres2017_257.html (last accessed 13.01.2020)

Viering, Markus G. et al. (2007): *Managementleistungen im Lebenszyklus von Immobilien*. 1. Auflage. Wiesbaden: Teubner, GWV Fachverlage

Wikipedia (2016): *Fédération Internationale des Administrateurs de Biens Conseils Immobiliers*. https://de.wikipedia.org/wiki/F%C3%A9d%C3%A9ration_Internationale_des_Administrateurs_de_Biens_Conseils_Immobiliers (last accessed: 13.01.2020)

Wikipedia (2017a): *Appraisal Institute*. https://en.wikipedia.org/wiki/Appraisal_Institute (last accessed 13.01.2020)

Wikipedia (2017b): *Hauptverband der allgemein beeideten und gerichtlich zertifizierten Gerichtssachverständigen*. https://de.wikipedia.org/wiki/Hauptverband_der_allgemein_beeideten_und_gerichtlich_zertifizierten_Gerichtssachverst%C3%A4ndigen (last accessed 26.01.2017)

Wikipedia (2017c): *Royal Institute of Chartered Surveyors*. https://de.wikipedia.org/wiki/Royal_Institution_of_Chartered_Surveyors (last accessed 13.01.2020)

Wikipedia (2017d): *Urban Land Institute*. https://de.wikipedia.org/wiki/Urban_Land_Institute (last accessed 13.01.2020)

WKÖ & Kranewitter, Heimo (2011): *Liegenschaftsbewertung*. http://public.wuapaa.com/wkk/2011/information_consulting/immobilien/files/Liegenschaftsbewertung.pdf (last accessed 26.04.2017)

Wofford, Larry et al. (2011): Real Estate Valuation, Cognitive Risk, and Translational Research. *Journal of Property Investment and Finance*. Vol. 29. No. 4–5

Wolverton, Marvin L. & Gallimore, Paul (1999): Client Feedback and the Role of the Appraiser. *Journal of Real Estate Research*. Vol. 18. No. 3

3 Conducting the study

52 interviews with appraisers, brokers, and owners

3.1. Interview setup

The interviews with real estate market actors were conducted between October 2017 and March 2018 via conference calls and face-to-face interviews. Out of 52 interviews, 23 of them were face-to-face and the rest were conference calls. The statements regarding the relative anonymity perceived by the interview partners can be confirmed after the experience of these 52 in-depth interviews, whereas it is worth mentioning that a much more important ingredient than a partial anonymity or a personal approach is the degree of trustworthiness perceived by the interview partner towards the interviewer, especially when conducting anonymized studies.

An interview may take place by phone or in person, but it is the degree of trust that matters for the validity of the outcome of a research project through in-depth interviews. The trust between the interviewer and the interviewee is the main ingredient for the success of a qualitative research project. In addition, the conducted interviews once again revealed confirmation concerning the validity given by the anonymized in-depth interviews. This type of interviewing was appropriate, especially for exploring the sensitive topics studied in this work, since the actors were not willing to disclose most of their insights in an open environment.

The interview schedule was designed for two main groups of the real estate market actors: for investors and developers (clients) and for brokers and appraisers (advisors). To implement a comprehensive research design in the work, qualitative data analysis was employed, with the aim to shed light on the behavior of the real estate market actors.

This study will present the individual actions from an institutional perspective via personal expert interviews with real estate investors and developers, as well as brokers and advisors. The interviews were conducted with decision-makers in the European real estate market, with a focus on Austria and Central Eastern Europe.

The research process was carried out through qualitative expert interviews, using the software-based NVivo (QSR International 2002) method. Buber und

Holzmüller (2009: 986) explain that the NVivo analysis software is suitable for "international market researchers conducting interviews with experts from several countries."

A solid catalog of questions was designed based on theoretical foundations and the phases of valuation as well as transaction processes. During the question generation phase, two categories of real estate market actors received particular attention: real estate brokers and appraisers and real estate investors and project developers. They were selected as follows:

- 24 real estate brokers and appraisers who work in small, medium-sized and large companies and have more than 10 years of experience in commercial real estate.
- 28 real estate investors and project developers who have experience will all three asset classes (retail, office and logistics real estate).

A robust catalog of questions was created for the 52 market actors that consisted of the following topics:

- For the real estate brokers and appraisers:
    - Advantages of being a member in a national or international real estate organization.
    - General opinions on real estate organizations, especially related to the ethics part and personal or company benefits.
    - The main interest when conducting a transaction.
    - Partnership with the investor before and after a transaction, including interests, behavior, differences in behavior depending on the investor's expertise on the specific market.
    - Asset valuation: Attempts to change or steer the valuation outcome before a transaction.
    - Brokers: Information disclosed before the deal and after it.
    - Appraisers: Flexibility margin, importance of the client's feedback.
    - Generic value drivers in the real estate business.
- For the investors:
    - Advantages of being a member in a national or international real estate organization.
    - General opinions on real estate organizations, especially related to the ethics and personal or company benefits.
    - The main interest when conducting a transaction.
    - Valuation process: How often appraisers are changed.
    - Contact with the appraiser between valuations.
    - Information not shared with the broker or with the appraiser during a transaction.
    - Generic value drivers in the real estate business.

The interviews were carried out in person and via conference calls, and then anonymized, so as to allow a solid trust foundation.

3.2. Data collection method and the issue of ethics

Increasingly, researchers are recognizing the benefits of research design that include qualitative methods to gain a deeper understanding and insights on complex issues and research phenomena. But one should consider the epistemological perspectives when designing a qualitative research study in order "to ensure consistency among research questions, the research approach, the methods, and the data analysis" (Van Note Chism 2008: 2).

The main motive for conducting qualitative research should be that "a research question requires the use of this sort of approach and not a different one" (Flick 2014: 12). It has less to do with finding the phenomena in the field than into "turning it into something that we can analyze" (Flick 2018: 7).

Further on, choosing a research technique depends on the readiness to accept the assumptions subject to each set of tools. Researchers who use tools and techniques underlining sizes and counting are called positivists; those who use the qualitative methods of observation, questioning, and conducting interviews are called naturalists.

Flick (2018: 7) outlines the common core of qualitative research by giving a general definition:

> Qualitative data collection is the selection and production of linguistic (or visual) material for analyzing and understanding phenomena, social fields, subjective and collective experiences and the related meaning-making processes. . . . It can be based on talking, listening, observing, analyzing materials as sounds, images or digital phenomena. Data collection can include single or multiple methods. The aim is often to arrive at materials that allow for producing generalizable statements by analyzing and comparing various exemplars, phenomena or cases.

The core values in qualitative research are described by "non-deception, non-discrimination, non-maleficence and beneficence" (Warnock 1971 in Bryman 2007b Vol. 1: 267). In other words, researchers should ensure they own integrity with their interview partners, that the data is property of the participant and it shall not be used for third-party purposes, that confidentiality must be respected, and that the will of a potential participant to not take part in a certain study is respected (Bryman 2007b Vol. 1: 277–279).

A key term in the ethical responsibilities towards the interview partner is informed consent, which is "ensuring that the actors understand the nature of the research, are aware of the risks it poses, and are not forced either covertly or overtly to participate" (Rubin & Rubin 2012: 91). It "entails informing actors about the overall purpose of the investigation and the main features of the design . . . [it] involves obtaining the voluntary participation of the people involved" (Kvale & Brinkmann 2009: 72).

Confidentiality as an ethical field in research implies that private data identifying the actors will not be disclosed and published (Kvale & Brinkmann 2009: 72–73), but this term might be inconsistent because keeping the material "confidential" means that no one but the interviewer would see it; instead, it should be referred to the maintaining the confidentiality of the actors' names and that original records such as transcripts should be kept in a secured place (Seidman 2013: 72–73).

To sum up, in qualitative research, the interviewer should note the dimension of the ethical sensitivity of the interviews he conducts and should ensure that the interviewee understands what the research is about, the purpose of the research, and that the answers are to be treated with confidentiality.

The interviews conducted in this work can be classified as *in-depth, elite interviews*. The advantage of in-depth interviews is that the detailed manner in which the interview is conducted allows the researcher to see how peoples' "experiences interact with powerful social and organizational forces that pervade the context in which they live and work, and we can discover the interconnections among people who live and work in a shared context" (Seidman 2013: 144).

Elite interviews are with leaders or experts in a certain field, usually in powerful positions, and obtaining access to them may be a key problem (Hertz & Imber 1995 in Kvale & Brinkmann 2009: 147). The expert and the elite interviewees are "agents of truth and authority increasingly dominating political decision-making in modern societies" (Flick 2018: 655).

There is no standard procedure for analyzing experts and elite interviews; basically, all qualitative research analysis methods can be used (code-based procedures from grounded theory, qualitative content analysis, sequential analysis or a combination of different methods). However, the suitable form of conducting and analyzing an expert interview depends on the research projects and its goals (Flick 2018: 664).

"Saturation" is the common term used to describe the moment one should stop sampling – it specifies to stop interviewing when including more cases does not contribute to any new information about the concepts developed (Schwandt 2001: 111 in Flick 2018: 90). In addition, Charmaz (2006: 113) concludes that the concepts are saturated in a qualitative research project as soon as "gathering fresh data no longer sparks new theoretical insights, nor reveals new properties of your core theoretical categories."

Finally, "partial anonymity granted by the telephone may increase the validity of responses by reducing the embarrassment involved in responding to emotionally or socially loaded questions in a face-to-face discussion" (Fenig et al. 1993 in Bryman 2007b Vol. 1: 38). "Our results suggest that the telephone can be an excellent screening method; the scores obtained correlated highly with those elicited in face-to-face interviews," as Fenig et al. (1993: 897) mention.

3.3. Data analysis

Qualitative Data Analysis (QDA) appears to have real advantages when conducting qualitative studies. As Weitzman (2000: 806) explains, the "real hopes" when using the QDA software are because it speeds up the process of handling and analyzing the data.

NVivo (used for this study as QDA tool for consolidating the qualitative information) is an electronic project which supports qualitative data and stores it with the scope of reflecting on the ideas and writing the findings. The program has tools to organize data (sources), to organize thoughts about data (codes), to support data (memos), and to explore it.

NVivo uses a specific vocabulary, and the most important key concepts can be summarized as follows:

- Sources: Research materials to be imported, the input.
- Nodes or codes: Generic term for containers related to themes, people, and units of observation.
- Cases: Different types of nodes with different functions.
- Classification: Descriptive information for the variables in the study.
- Collections: Group different items in a set, for example two organizations.
- Queries: The output.

In this study, the *sources* consist of the Word files with the 52 interview transcripts, the *nodes* are organized into two categories of the interview partners (Advisor and Client) that are further anonymized and labeled according to the experience with the certain asset class and number of interview (e.g., PLO09 is a Client with experience in the logistics and office real estate market, interview number 9). Finally, the *classification* in NVivo was done according to company size, country, membership in a real estate organization, and public company.

The purpose of this study is to investigate the interests, motivations, and actions of real estate service providers and clients on the real estate market, as well as to shed light on relevant issues in the valuation process of commercial property. Furthermore, the scope of action for the market actors, as well as the decisional bandwidths for property appraisers, are presented and linked to the theory of Behavioral Real Estate and information asymmetries.

To examine these issues, besides the qualitative analysis in NVivo, simulations were conducted with the chi-squared test, as well as with the logistic regression, to explore the relationships between the two categories of real estate market actors, real estate service providers, and clients.

In short, the chi-squared test can be used to assert and verify possible relationships between two categorical variables by designing a two-way table in which the observed outcome is compared to the expected counts of the cells. As Moore and McCabe (2003: 624) illustrate, the "chi-square statistic is a measure of how much the observed cell counts in a two-way table diverge from the expected cell counts."

The chi-square test begins with the following hypothesis (Yamane 1976: 648–651):

> Ho: Row and column variables are independent, there is no relationship between the variables
> Ha: Row and column variables are not independent, there is a relationship between the variables

When the difference between the expected outcome and the observed one is substantial, the evidence is against the null hypothesis and in favor of the alternative one.

In addition to the chi-square test, the logistic regression (also called logit model), a widely used multivariable method for modeling dichotomous outcomes, was used to analyze the relationships of the real estate market actors more deeply, as previously explained. This was facilitated by the software package for statistics and data science called STATA, which is mostly used for economics and sociology research.

Furthermore, Sperandei (2014) illustrates and explains the rationale of the logistics regression procedure:

> Logistic regression works very similar to linear regression, but with a binomial response variable . . . you can use continuous explanatory variables and it is easier to handle more than two explanatory variables simultaneously. Although apparently trivial, this last characteristic is essential when we are interested in the impact of various explanatory variables on the response variable.

The following chapter will show the results related to the interests and opinions of the market actors related to real estate organizations, as well as findings in Behavioral Real Estate.

Bibliography

Adler, Patricia & Adler, Peter (2012): The Epistemology of Numbers, in Baker, Sarah & Edwards, Rosalind (eds.) *How Many Qualitative Interviews Is Enough? Expert Voices and Career Reflections on Sampling and Cases in Qualitative Research.* National Center for Research Methods. ESRC Economic & Social Research Council. http://eprints.ncrm.ac.uk/2273/4/how_many_interviews.pdf

Bryman, Alan (2007a): *Qualitative Research 2*. Vol. II. Quality Issues in Qualitative Research. London: Sage Publications

Bryman, Alan (2007b): *Qualitative Research 2*. Vol. I. Collecting Data for Qualitative Research. London: Sage Publications

Buber, Renate & Holzmüller, Hartmut H. (2009): *Qualitative Marktforschung. Konzepte – Methoden – Analyse.* Band 2. Überbearbeitete Auflage. Wiesbaden: Gabler GWV Fachverlage

Charmaz, Kathy (2006): *Constructing Grounded Theory: A Practical Guide Through Qualitative Analysis.* London: Sage Publications

Doucet, Andrea (2012): *How Many Qualitative Interviews Is Enough? Expert Voices and Career Reflections on Sampling and Cases in Qualitative Research.* Baker, Sarah & Edwards, Rosalind (eds.). National Center for Research Methods. ESRC Economic & Social Research Council. http://eprints.ncrm.ac.uk/2273/4/how_many_interviews.pdf

Fenig, Shmuel et al. (1993): Telephone vs Face-to-Face Interviewing in a Community Psychiatric Survey. *American Journal of Public Health*. Vol. 83. No. 6. PP. 896–898.

Flick, Uwe (2007): *Qualitative Sozialforschung. Eine Einführung*. Reinbek bei Hamburg: Rowohlt Taschenbuch Verlag

Flick, Uwe (2014): *An Introduction to Qualitative Research*. Fifth Edition. London: Sage Publications

Flick, Uwe (2018): *The Sage Book of Qualitative Data Collection*. London: Sage Publications

Fusch, Patricia & Ness, Lawrence R. (2015): *Are We There Yet?* Data Saturation in Qualitative Research. *The Qualitative Report*. Vol. 20. No. 9. https://nsuworks.nova.edu/tqr/vol20/iss9/3/ (last accessed 20.01.2020)

Hertz, Rosanna & Imber, Jonathan B. (1995): *Studying Elites Using Qualitative Methods. A Sage Focus Edition*. Thousand Oaks, CA: Sage Publications Inc. Except Chapter 3 1990 by Human Sciences Press and Chapter 4 1992 by Human Sciences Press

Kvale, Steinar (1996): *Interviews: An Introduction to Qualitative Research Interviewing*. Thousand Oaks: Sage Publications

Kvale, Steinar & Brinkmann, Svend (2009): *Interviews: Learning the Craft of Qualitative Research Interviewing*. Second Edition. London: Sage Publications

Marshall, Catherine & Rossman, Gretchen B. (1989): *Designing Qualitative Research*. Newbury Park: Sage Publications

Mason, Mark (2010): Sample Size and Saturation in PhD Studies Using Qualitative Interviews. *Forum Qualitative Sozialforschung/Forum Qualitative Social Research*. Vol. 11, No. 3, Art. 8. Supported by the Institute for Qualitative Research and the Center for Digital Systems, Freie Universität Berlin

Moore, David S. & McCabe, George P. (2003): *Introduction to the Practice of Statistics*. New York: W. H. Freeman and Company

Morse, Janice M. (2000): Determining Sample Size. *Qualitative Health Research*. Vol. 10. No. 1. PP. 3–5

QSR International (2002): *Introducing NVivo: A Workshop Handbook*. www.nuigalway.ie/administration_services/stdo/crs_downloads/nvivo_workbook.pdf (last accessed 20.01.2020)

QSR International (2017): *NVivo 11 Pro for Windows: Getting Started Guide*.

Rubin, Herbert J. & Rubin, Irene S. (2012): *Qualitative Interviewing: The Art of Hearing Data*. Third Edition. Northern Illinois University. Thousand Oaks: Sage Publications

Schwandt, Thomas A. (2001): *Dictionary of Qualitative Inquiry*. Second Edition. Thousand Oaks, CA: Sage Publications

Seidman, Irving (2013): *Interviewing as Qualitative Research. A Guide for Researchers in Education and the Social Sciences*. Fourth Edition. Columbia University et al.: Teachers College Press

Sperandei, Sandro (2014): *Understanding Logistic Regression Analysis*. Zagreb: Biochem Med. www.ncbi.nlm.nih.gov/pmc/articles/PMC3936971/ (last accessed 20.01.2020)

Van Note Chism, Nancy et al. (2008): *Qualitative Research. Basics: A Guide for Engineering Educators*. Rigorous Research in Engineering Education. https://www.ncbi.nlm.nih.gov/pmc/articles/PMC3936971/ (last accessed: 28.05.2020)

Warnock, Geoffrey (1971): *The Object of Morality*. University paperbacks, 412. London: Methuen & Co Ltd.

Weitzman, Eben A. (2000): Software and Qualitative Research, in Denzin, Norman K. & Lincoln, Yvonna S. (eds.) *The Sage Handbook of Qualitative Research*. Second Edition. London: Sage Publications

Yamane, Taro (1976): *Statistik. Ein einführendes Lehrbuch*. Band 2. Frankfurt am Main: Fischer Taschenbuch Verlag

4 Findings for Behavioral Real Estate

4.1. Overview

This study provides a specific roadmap to merge qualitative research through expert interviews to the literature of Behavioral Economics and Agency theory, and thereby contributes to the findings on Behavioral Real Estate related to property valuation and appraisal, as well as to moral hazard in real estate.

Further, the work offers validation for previous research in the related areas of valuation and appraisal – smoothing, anchoring, client's feedback, valuation rationale – ensuring robustness of the final product and gaining an understanding of the complex issues influencing the triggers of the market actors in commercial property valuation.

The qualitative data was collected though in-depth interviews with market leaders and senior executives, and was afterwards used to gain qualitative feedback on:

- Potential information asymmetries between market actors in commercial property valuation.
- The value drivers of the real estate market actors, limited to real estate brokers, appraisers, and investors and developers.
- The behavior of the aforementioned market actors when valuating real estate properties for transaction purposes.
- Their opinion regarding real estate organizations in direct relationship to ethics.
- The cooperation and benefits the real estate market actors see in long-term business relationships.
- Valuation rationale from the investors' point of view.
- Valuation rationale from the appraisers' point of view, including smoothing and anchoring.
- The importance of client feedback for real estate brokers and appraisers.
- The differences real estate service providers make between the clients they have depending on company size, level of experience, or long-term business relationships.

4.2. The interests of market actors related to real estate organizations

4.2.1. Introduction

The following chapter will offer an overview of the different opinions and interests of the real estate market actors regarding memberships in different national and international real estate organizations.

Among the 52 interviewed market actors, 27 of them are members of real estate organizations, whereas most of the appraisers also have additional memberships with appraisers' associations in their country of residence.

The following chapter will present the results from the conducted interviews related to personal opinions of advisors (as appraisers and real estate brokers) and clients (investors) concerning the advantages they see for having memberships in real estate organizations, the reasons for not having or not needing to have a membership, the special case for advisors being members of appraisers' associations, and last but not least, the clients' and advisors' opinions related to the mandates which are given through the network of the real estate organizations or thorough other channels.

4.2.2. Advisors' opinions related to real estate organizations

4.2.2.1. Positive opinions of advisors

More of the half of the interviewed advisors consider memberships important for their personal career development as well as for the network or business ethics. The reasons vary based on the internationality of the business environment and on mandatory memberships in the case of appraisers.

The 18 positive opinions of the real estate advisors are split as follows: 13 advisors are already members of at least one organization, 10 of them are appraisers, 7 are brokers and 1 has the statute of both broker and appraiser. Moreover, 10 of the advisors come from large companies, one from a medium-sized company and the rest from small companies.

The positive opinions and interests for having a membership of the advisors who consider it important to have a membership in a national or international real estate organization can be divided into the following main categories:

- International environment.
- Business ethics and code of conduct.
- Signalize the professional standard.
- Education.
- Networking.

The internationality of the environment is highlighted especially by the interviewees from CEE countries, who state that it is important to be a member in an organization when dealing with international clients or when working in a corporate environment. Furthermore, the appraisers in CEE aim to have "the same label as in Western Europe."

Business ethics and the code of conduct instituted by the real estate organizations play an important role for the advisors, especially because they are relevant to the business partners they work with. Integrity and trust are two related criteria, as one tends "to trust more a member of a certain real estate organization, for that specific case, either on a national or on an international level."

The third reason why advisors find real estate organizations important is because they want to signalize their track record and their standards of business behavior by ensuring security for their business conduct. The credential and the title are important when dealing with clients who only want to work with reputable partners, either appraisers or real estate brokers.

Moreover, the appraisers highlight the importance of their memberships especially due to the valuation reports requested by institutional companies that need to be conducted based on RICS or IFRS standards. The "banks started to be more cautious after the crisis and tried to prevent the case of the bad loans for the future," as an appraiser from a large company discloses.

However, an additional argument for showing the expertise an advisor has is the company brand. According to one interview partner, real estate organizations "make only a quarter of the business, the rest is the brand of the company and what you have to offer."

Real estate education and career development are important factors when deciding on a membership in a real estate organization. On one hand, there are still countries without university-level education in real estate, in which case RICS might be an option for many market actors. One the other hand, the real estate organizations support the daily business of an appraiser with templates or other related documentation.

Networking is an essential argument for having a membership in a real estate organization. Besides the general statements such as "important to be seen," "get to know lots of people very fast," "exchange experience with colleagues," and "exchange information," there are opinions showing that through such

Figure 4.1 NVivo Word Cloud – Advisors' positive opinions related to organizations

networking, personal relationships are created, thus the image and the perception of other real estate market actors are considered highly significant.

Yet, the real estate organizations are regarded by brokers and appraisers at the same time as a "combination between network and clients." While the advisors mention they use such networks to get to potential clients or search for new employees, brokers make use of different associations that connect them to clients and facilitate a long-term business relationship because "once a client did a business with you, he will remain loyal and you have some kind of an exclusivity."

4.2.2.2. *Advisors' motives not to have a membership*

In this research, 10 of 28 advisors described the reasons why a membership in a national or international real estate organization is not relevant to them.

Before enumerating the motives, it is worth analyzing the background the advisors have: as regards the advisor type, 6 of them are brokers, the other 3 are brokers as well as appraisers, and one is only appraiser; 7 of them work at small and medium-sized companies, only 3 at large ones; 3 of them are members of a real estate organization, while the other 7 are not; they all have experience with all three asset classes relevant for this study – retail, office, and logistics.

To sum up, the advisors who do not find real estate organizations to be relevant for their business are those who come from smaller companies, with no memberships in a real estate organization, mainly brokers, with experience in all asset classes of commercial real estate.

The present research has revealed that the advisors who do not need any membership in a real estate organization are led by the following motives:

- Own network.
- Local environment.
- No direct professional advantage.
- Financial aspects.

The main reason which was described by the advisors for not having a membership in a real estate organization is their own network of business contacts, which is asserted to be more relevant than the contacts they would arrive at through real estate organizations: "I am a well-known broker on the local market and have my own contacts," "the same people you deal with," "time consuming, since I have my own network anyway," and "I have a business network of brokers around Europe, it is like an independent, closed club; we work professionally and target-oriented."

The local environment or local business is in fact linked to the main reason previously mentioned, that the advisors have their own network. Several statements from brokers show that their local networks play a much larger role than the contacts facilitated by international real estate organizations (e.g., RICS): "less relevant in a small country," "the informal networks work much better," "for small companies as mine such contacts and networks work faster," and "RICS makes sense on an international level, all other organizations are not interesting."

Furthermore, there are advisors who do not see any business or professional advantage connected to memberships in real estate organizations. The specified reason is connected to the fact that a real estate organization does not bring "immediate money," clients, or career improvement.

The appraisers have private clients or clients from operative foundations (germ. "Stiftung") who do not require a certain membership or do not want the appraiser "to be present and on focus." Also, the ethical issue was put in question by an appraiser who is also a broker: "the quality of my work increases because I do not have to comply with any other rule, I work according to my own business rules and ethics and this is appreciated by my clients." The same advisor also added, "from my experience, the big companies are not ethical at all – I mean their employees are not ethical."

On the other hand, despite the certain degree of skepticism related to real estate organizations, the real estate service providers also appreciate the importance of memberships in different real estate organizations, with the aim of signaling, thus (...) categories:

- Desire to be recognized on an international level ("when dealing with international clients this is very important").
- Display credentials ("the code of conduct plays a role for me and is relevant for my business partners"; "these titles and designations however help a lot in the relationship with my clients and with potential ones, I signalize that I am certified and that I am part of this business").
- Certifications ("for ImmoZert in Austria you have to renew your certification, I consider this is very important for the appraisers").
- Ethics ("represent integrity and a high degree of ethics").

Finally, financial aspects are also assessed when deciding upon having a membership. The advisors mention that "all this costs money" and they work anyway "according to their [the real estate organizations'] principles of business conduct," without having to pay any fee.

To sum up, most of the advisors – and here, especially, the real estate brokers – from small companies do not show a direct interest of being members of national or international real estate organization.

4.2.3. *Clients' opinions related to real estate organizations*

4.2.3.1. Positive opinions of clients

The opinions related to real estate organizations that came from the clients' side are split, and only half of the interview participants see a membership as an advantage: 3 of the 12 clients come from public companies; 9 of them are active members of at least one real estate organization, the other 3 are not; 8 clients come from small and medium-sized companies, while 4 of them work for large companies; and 3 of the clients are active only in the logistics sector, 1 of them in the retail sector, and the rest have experience with all three asset classes (retail, office, logistics).

The interviews conducted with the clients reveal that their positive opinions related to real estate organizations are similar to the advisors' opinions, and they can be classified into five main categories:

- Networking; information exchange.
- International environment.
- Education.
- Values represented by real estate organizations.
- Career development.

The networking as well as the information exchange facilitated through the meetings and events organized by different real estate organizations play a significant role for the clients. A membership in a real estate organization eases the access to certain information (e.g., projects in the pipeline, latest information on the market, contacts, personal introduction, recommendations, know-how, etc.) and helps networking as well as building confidence in the other market actors with the same background.

Moreover, through such channels, a certain level of informality and confidentiality are created, since the members belong to the same circle of interests. The real estate organizations have also a "voice function" related to recent market developments.

The second important factor when deciding to have a membership in a real estate organization is the international aspect. Several clients mentioned the advantage and extended perspectives RICS can contribute to when working in an international real estate business environment. In fact, RICS is the only real estate organization with a direct connection to an international environment.

Besides the exchange of experience previously mentioned, the continuing education offered by real estate organizations is a plus for the real estate market actors. The market knowledge, training, and lifelong learning encouraged by most real estate organizations constitute an important factor for deciding upon a membership in a real estate organization.

In this regard, RICS is again given as a positive example since its members are "forced to go to events or do seminars, because each year you have to have a minimum number of hours spent in developing your career." Another interview participant conceded that

> it is very important especially in the markets we work with, we need more specialists to speak the same language; I learned by doing . . . I do not have real estate studies, but I encourage the new generation and the young professionals to do that.

Figure 4.2 NVivo Word Cloud – Clients' positive opinions related to organizations

A further reason for clients to have positive opinions regarding real estate organizations involves the values that these organizations generally represent. Clients identify values connected to transparency, seriousness, business ethics, confidentiality, and professionalism.

The real estate market actors want to be "seen and respected as a real estate professional." This is why "recognition," "image," and "reputation" are also aspects that stay in a direct connection to these values; the real estate organizations "filter the real estate market players, by creating an environment and a network of professionals" while pledging for a "certain quality criteria."

In addition to that, career development is a significant component for memberships. The importance concerning job opportunities facilitated by real estate organizations is relevant as well: "if I were to leave my current job, I would definitely look here for new perspectives." Nevertheless, the payment of the membership fee might be put into question if the company did not pay it: "personally, it would make a difference if I had to pay the fee myself; now the company pays it."

4.2.3.2. Clients' motives not to have a membership

As previously mentioned, the opinions with respect to real estate organizations and the related memberships in such organizations are split in half. While 12 of the interview partners mention the positive aspects and the reasons why they find such organizations relevant for the real estate business, the other 12 explain their motives for not choosing to be a member of a real estate organization.

The clients who do not find real estate organizations relevant for their daily business come from small (4), medium-sized (3), and large (5) companies; 11 of them are not members of any real estate organization; 4 work in public companies; and all of them invest in the three asset classes – retail, office, and logistics.

The argument of the clients for not having a membership in a real estate organization is similar to that of the advisors. Parameters such as their own network or local business environment are relevant milestones for deciding not to have a membership, but there are also other motives that the clients could be identified with. The reasons why the clients do not opt for memberships in real estate organizations can be divided into the following generic categories:

- Own network.
- Local environment.
- Type of business.
- Company size.
- No direct professional advantage.
- Substitutes.

The rationale of having their own network resembles the opinions of the advisors. The accent is mostly put on invitations to real estate events, but also on the "direct contact" to the business partners "outside the real estate organizations."

Another consideration for not needing to have a membership is illustrated by the local environment. The real estate organizations are not active or well-known in certain local real estate markets. Furthermore, the clients who invest in logistics real estate point out that the real estate organizations aren't relevant to them: "logistics is a special asset class and we work very regional, so this kind of real estate networks – national or international – are not relevant to us."

Furthermore, the type of business is directly related to the fact that some clients do not need memberships in real estate organizations. The clients mention that a difference should be made between them and the brokers and appraisers who indeed need such memberships to acquire clients. According to the opinion of one interview partner, there is no need for him as client to be part of a real estate organization because he considers himself to be a "consumer of the real estate services."

Company size is a further argument for clients who do not consider real estate organizations relevant to their business. They make a contrast between the small companies which "are not in such big real estate organizations" or family offices versus big, international companies, where a membership is not needed due to the business contacts that are already available: "the notoriety of my company is enough for me," or "I try to have my own network and since we are on an institutional level, we have any contact we need."

Analogous to the advisors, there are also clients who do not consider that a real estate organization brings a direct professional advantage. The evidence for these arguments comes from statements such as "a membership should be seen as a quality feature of those who have it, but this does not mean that it necessarily brings an advantage" and "I must say it does not bring so much; it is so to say nice for the business card."

There are clients who regard commercial real estate services and investment firms as substitutes for real estate organizations. The international agencies are sometimes used for information exchange, for benchmarking and market analysis,

Figure 4.3 NVivo Word Cloud – Mandatory and non-mandatory organizations

and valuation and brokerage services, especially in the logistics sector. In this manner, the international expertise is combined with networking and provision of real estate services.

4.2.4. Mandates received through real estate organizations

4.2.4.1. Advisors' experience

A total of 11 brokers and appraisers who have experience with all commercial real estate asset classes find it convenient to use real estate associations for approaching potential clients. Seven of them work in small and medium-sized companies, the rest in large companies, and 8 of them are members in a real estate organization.

From the appraisers' perspective, real estate networks are often used to get in direct contact with potential customers: "mandates coming through such organizations and networks are again a side effect, in an inherent manner; from the business approach you develop a personal network, and this leads to further mandates."

Another appraiser points out that the first personal contact with clients is "at events organized by the real estate organizations, we keep in touch, and this is how they come back when they have a mandate."

By contrast, 8 advisors – 5 of them already members of real estate associations – explain that they do not find it relevant to use real estate organizations for receiving mandates or approaching potential clients, mainly due to the fact that they use their "private network" and recommendations, or just because there is no need when they already have a valuation department in the company they work for.

4.2.4.2. Clients' experience

Few clients utter a positive opinion concerning mandates facilitated by contacts from real estate organizations. Only 3 out of 24 interviewees, working for small,

Figure 4.4 NVivo Word Cloud – Mandates received through organizations

medium, and large public and non-public companies, consider approaching an appraiser through a real estate organization (e.g., RICS). Still, such a contact should be seen "only on an international basis," not on a national level, and here RICS can be a "powerful network." Furthermore, a client explains that the "title makes no importance nationally speaking, here in Austria; on an international level, the title makes a difference."

Another case when a client searches for a service provider through a real estate organization is "when you enter a complete new market."

Apart from searching an appraiser or a broker though a national or international real estate network, there are clients who highlight the importance of direct contact with their appraisers in order to "create a trustworthy basis with them and have something to say about the valuation result." In this sense, a direct contact to the appraiser through a real estate network might not be so important, as another client affirms: "I want to know the appraiser better (and this is not exactly happening through networks, but through personal business relationships), be able to have a conversation basis with him and exchange recommendations and opinions."

Analogous to the advisors, the clients find their own network to be more powerful when searching for an appraiser: "I revert again to my network and the personal experience I had so far with different appraisers," "the market reputation plays a role for me, so I never use the real estate networks in a direct way," and "I always find appraisers from a personal connection and in my opinion they should always work for large, renowned organizations." Alternatively, clients also choose to "go directly to the big companies anyway and they already have such memberships and titles."

Also, the banks play a significant role when deciding upon a valuation mandate. A client mentions that this "is a quality standard for a bank which finances you; the bank normally accepts only valuation reports from big companies which are well-known on the market."

Further reasons clients do not search for real estate advisors in a direct way are because of the company board "picking the appraiser is a Board decision" and there being "no need to search them through such a network, since my companies have been chosen them."

A last argument that clients give in explaining why they do not use real estate organizations for contacting appraisers is the situation of an investment fund,

Figure 4.5 NVivo Word Cloud – No mandates through organizations

when the financial supervisory authority names the appraisers the investment fund is entitled to work with. A client annotates the following:

> as we operate under the Germany fund rules, even though we are based in Austria, we have to respect their [the German Federal Financial Supervisory Authority] rules of procedures regarding the assignment of the appraisers; the main issue is the insurance amount the appraisers are willing to give; most of them work with low amounts and for a real estate investment fund like us most of the appraisers do not comply with our requirements.

4.3. Preliminary results related to real estate organizations

4.3.1. *Results of the qualitative analysis*

The target of this work is to identify behaviors underlying the construct of interest of the real estate market actors – clients as well as service providers. Part of the original motivation for this study was to formalize the ethics issue in business relationships between the market actors and investigate whether the ethics principles of real estate organizations play a significant role for the appraisers, real estate brokers, and investors.

First, the analysis presented in the previous sections reveals that both categories of market actors (clients and service providers) illustrate similar motives to be part of a real estate organization. These motives can be structured as follows:

1 When acting in an *international business environment*, a membership in an international organization is beneficial. This fact is argued mostly by the market actors from Central and Eastern Europe, and less by those active on the real estate market.
2 The *values* represented by real estate organizations play a notable role for the market actors; business ethics, code of conduct, confidentiality, professionalism, and transparency are the most used terms.

3 *Networking* as well as information exchange between market actors.
4 *Education* and continuous career development.
5 The service providers aim to *signalize* the professional standard they want to represent. Furthermore, the appraisers (depending on the country and type of activity) need to be part of certain appraisers' organizations.

To sum up, in the international or institutional business environment, the values represented by real estate organizations, networking, and a continuous education as well as signalizing are the main motives of the real estate market actors to decide upon a membership in a real estate organization.

By contrast, considerations such as personal network, local business environment, no business advantage, financial aspects, and substitutes play a role for real estate brokers, appraisers, and investors to not opt for a membership, and, in a first instance at least, not to stand for the aforementioned values. These can be summarized as follows:

1 The existence of a *strong personal network*.
2 *Local business environment*, no internationality (e.g., family offices).
3 *No direct business advantage*, no direct mandates or businesses undertaken because of the memberships.
4 *Financial aspects*, membership costs.
5 *Substitutes*: international agencies instead of organizations.

The second part of this chapter revealed a deeper understanding of the advisors' perspectives related to the mandates received through real estate organizations. While private networks (....) are the main reasons why the service providers do not need to search for mandates through real estate associations, there are other advisors who make use of such organizations in order to reach out to potential clients (e.g. at events, networking), whereas established networks might enable the acquisition of new client opportunities.

4.3.2. Results of the quantitative analysis

The next section aims to develop quantitative findings of the undertaken interviews with the 52 market actors. The analysis has been split in two areas, on one hand the behavior and opinions towards real estate organizations; on the other hand, the evidence specifically related to three main pillars of Behavioral Real Estate: valuation rationale, valuation anchoring, and client's feedback. The chi-squared test and the logistic regression have been used to investigate the quantitative findings using binary models with a dependent variable with two possible values.

The results of the two quantitative methods brought strong evidence related to the behavior and the perception of the real estate market actors towards real estate organizations; however, due to a relatively small number of cases, the quantitative analysis in the field of Behavioral Real Estate (as previously presented) could not lead to a significant, quantifiable outcome. Possible influences were considered, but they did not turn out to be significant because of a rather low number of cases for a quantitative study.

The input data used for investigating the quantitative results with the chi-squared test, as well as with the logistic regression, are represented in the Annexes of this work.

First, the chi-squared test was used for the investigation of the market actors' opinions towards real estate organizations. The market actors have been split in the two main categories, client and advisor, whereas the former category has been also divided into two sub-categories, broker and appraiser. The target of this method was to investigate the cases that reach a significance level of above 95% to achieve a significant statistic evidence.

The result of the chi-squared test indicates strong evidence related to the opinions of the market actors towards real estate organizations in two main areas: there is a strong positive relationship between the variables "advisor type" and "positive (1)/negative (0) opinion," as well as related to the variables "positive (1)/negative (0) opinion" and "member."

Due to a positive result for a significant relationship between the aforementioned variables, it may be inferred that the appraisers have a tendency to express positive opinions towards memberships in real estate organizations and the benefits related to such a membership, while the real estate brokers do not assess memberships in a real estate organization in such a positive manner.

The result of the chi-squared test also leads to evidence of a positive relationship between the market actors' opinions (positive [1]/negative [0]) and their memberships; hence, while the members of real estate organizations (clients as well as advisors) generally assess memberships in a positive manner, those who are not members yet do not articulate such a strong positive experience or opinions related to real estate organizations.

Chi-squared test

1 Opinion and advisor type: After conducting the chi-squared test, there is a significance level of 97.43%, meaning a significant relationship between positive/negative opinions related to real estate organizations and advisor type.
2 Opinion and member: After conducting the chi-squared test, there in a significance level of 98.24%, meaning a significant relationship between positive/negative opinions related to real estate organizations and memberships.

Logistic regression

Second, the results of the logistic regression model conducted indicate the following evidence related to the opinions of the real estate market actors towards memberships in real estate organizations.

The logistic regression was analyzed with STATA, the software package used in the field of economics that can provide statistical analysis and regression beyond data structure and storage management. The gradation was made as follows: the positive opinions related to real estate organizations ("yes") were graded with "1," the negative opinions ("no") were graded with "0," and the missing values were graded with "-99."

All three logistic regression models show a number of 52 cases where Pseudo R2 (the square of the correlation between predicted and actual value, ranging from 0 to 1) is around 0.3. Moreover, "n_member" is the lowest value (0.001, 0.002), showing that the membership is the only variable which is significant when analyzing the opinions of the real estate market actors related to real estate organizations.

The other variables (company size, advisor type, public company, company size) do not show any significance in the conducted logistic regression.

The positive opinions of the market actors are connected to the "membership" status in a direct manner; when "membership" is positive ("1"), the tendency to express a positive opinion related to real estate organizations is positive as well.

To sum up, membership status is the single relevant variable, whereas the others, such as company size, advisor type, type of company, and company size, are not significant.

The result of the logistic regression can lead to the argument that the real estate market actors have positive opinions about organizations when they already have a membership status in at least one real estate organization or association.

4.4. Behavioral Real Estate

4.4.1. Introduction

This work is an attempt to shed light and provide further evidence to Behavioral Real Estate in commercial property valuation for transaction purposes. The findings are consistent with previous behavioral studies, which suggest that the relationship between appraisers and their clients might influence the outcome of the valuation process. The research conducted through in-depth interviews with 52 real estate market actors focuses on two things: on one hand, on revealing which type of influence exists and to which extent; on the other hand, it tries to illustrate the flexibility margins of clients and service providers when valuating real estate properties.

In the next section, the result of the qualitative research done through in-depth interviews with 52 interviewees describes the behavioral perspective of the market actors in commercial property valuation. The main topics of the interviews conducted tackled areas such as: main interests when conducting a transaction and generic value drivers, partnership between clients and service providers before and after a transaction or a valuation mandate (including interests, behavior and information exchange, flexibility margins at property valuations, and limits), the importance of the client's feedback, and, finally, how often appraisers are changed and whether any contact with them exists between valuations.

Based on the literature related to Behavioral Real Estate Economics, the structure of the rest of the section is made up as follows: firstly, the *valuation rationale* from the market actors' perspective is illustrated. This includes evidence on the *pressure put on appraisers* as well as an illustration on the parameters that can influence the valuation outcome, seen from both perspectives: clients and advisors.

Furthermore, the research also revealed that besides the appraisers, real estate brokers, and investors, there is an additional category of market actors who might play a significant role in the valuation process, especially on an institutional level.

The following section provides a deeper evidence on *valuation anchoring*, on the relationships between clients, and service providers and the distinctions each party undertakes, including the importance of *client's feedback* in commercial property valuation. The section will finally provide a closing note on the concrete *value drivers* of the market actors.

4.4.2. *Valuation rationale*

4.4.2.1. *Brokers' opinions and behavior related to valuation*

The following section outlines the aspects of property valuation seen from the perspective of the commercial real estate brokers, who try to illustrate why they find valuations to be subjective and strive to convince their clients to accept a certain value or price, with the purpose of having a successful transaction.

Moreover, the brokers interviewed also explain why they have to refuse mandates for the commercialization of a certain commercial property. Finally, the perspective of the brokers who work for international real estate advisory companies will be also presented as an attempt to envisage the relationship and communication with their in-house valuation department.

Among the 52 interview partners, 16 of them are brokers with more than 10 years of experience in commercial real estate transactions. A couple of the brokers active in this international environment compare their profession to that of an advisor, and claim they are a "mirror of the market" by looking at "comparable transactions in the region" and trying not to exaggerate when it comes to steering a real estate transaction.

Still, the commercial real estate brokers share similar opinions related to valuations for transaction purposes. They consider valuations to be "subjective," while there is "a big pressure put on the appraisers" as the "clients always want to receive certain numbers." Nevertheless, a broker who has expertise on the Romanian real estate market and works for an international brokerage and advisory company observes that almost all institutional investors in Romania need professional market and valuation reports, and these companies can be "rather inflexible, because of the bad image from the past, when valuations were not so correct."

Other brokers envisaged their opinions about the subjectivity of valuations by stating that "the value of the property is what you can do with it" or "valuation is not a fixed amount, you can justify it within a certain interval depending on the yield."

In the following section, 12 real estate brokers coming from small (6), large (5), and medium-sized (1) companies, try to unfold their motives for persuading their clients to lower the price expectations or to even decline transaction mandates, with the justification that the targeted sale price is not realistic. Only one quarter of the brokers who offer such opinions are members of real estate organizations.

The real estate brokers try to adapt to the requests and expectations of their clients when it comes to the commercialization of a property; however, this happens "up to a certain point that I can represent" as a broker from Romania working for an international corporation mentions.

Additionally, another broker completes by saying:

> there are some big companies who have clear practices and guidelines, for example not to sell at a value of more than +20%; in this case we adapt and correct downwards; we want to maintain a good relationship with the client, we can adapt but we do not want to exaggerate; we want to attenuate, to stabilize the expectations of the clients we have, so adaptation is best the word.

The yield and the book value are the main parameters the real estate brokers look at and try to negotiate with their clients. As the property value and, most important of all, the sale price, depend on that, the brokers emphasize the importance of explaining or even convincing clients about their own view of the market price:

- "I point out to my client if the value is wrong in my opinion."
- "I try to convince the investor that the market value should be lower, in order to get the deal done."
- "Book values are important for big companies; the smaller ones can 'rearrange' the book value or even accept a certain loss, so sometimes I manage to convince the investors to lower the book value."
- "If a lot of time goes by and the property was not sold, I also try to convince the client to lower the book value."
- "My role is therefore to talk about the yield and explain it."
- "I know cases when the price was valuated much too high, especially before the crisis. I try to make my clients aware of that and explain the value is lower."
- "I am also an appraiser, so I can give concrete details; most of the time the investor comes to me after half a year and is ready to drop down the value or the price expectations, in order to do the deal."

Another real estate broker, working for an international brokerage and advisory company, explains the importance of the brokerage agreements and the fact that these should be signed before a transaction, even though the initial price expectation of an investor does not coincide to his own opinion:

> There are owners who expect to sell at let's say 45 Euro per square meter, although we say this is much above the market. We tell the owner that we do not know anyone to pay so much for a land in that specific location. We say to ourselves 'we lose our time but ok, let's give it a try.' And then we sign the brokerage agreement, which is important for us. Time goes by, the offers (normally much lower) come, the owner (our client) starts to negotiate after a while and we finally come to an agreement. It would work like that: the owner says 45 Euro, we sign the brokerage agreement anyway, the best offer is 28 Euro, the owner says 33 and so we can meet in the middle at 30 Euro per square meter. So, it takes time, but the brokerage agreement is important to be signed.

However, there are certain circumstances when the real estate brokers might immediately decline a transaction mandate, since a "property must be sellable." Here, the property value is the most important factor, and there are brokers who turn down a mandate and "lose clients or contracts" because they do not want to "adapt to certain requests." In the following, there are several opinions which portray such cases:

- "If there are differences between valuation assumptions and expectations as compared to the real market, I do not want to go on that road."
- "I normally take the DCF [discounted cash-flow] calculation and look at it, in order to see what the assumptions are; if they are exaggerated, I decline the mandate."
- "I know of other brokers who do that, who do not decline a mandate even though they know it is overpriced."
- "I would not accept a property which has a value of 3 M. Euro, but the market price is 2.5 M Euro, unless the investor accepts such a decrease."

A noteworthy remark related to brokers trying to convince their clients about a certain transaction price comes from an advisor (broker as well as appraiser) who works for a small company in Austria:

> I am flexible, of course. But I am also honest, and I want to avoid a pointless effort. For example, an investor once had an exaggerated expectation in my view. He wanted to receive a price of X M. Euro. I found that totally excessive. When such thing happens, I am not interested because I know I would work in vain. But I went to a potential buyer and told him like that: 'consider this X M. Euro is a joke. My price and my truth is X minus 13 M.' The parties seem to have accepted that and they are now in the Due Diligence process. So, I always try to be transparent in order not to lose time.

Furthermore, a couple of brokers with extended experience in commercial real estate try to differentiate between the asset classes in their attempt to explain their own views to potential investors. While industrial and logistics, or even retail properties, are more complex, there might be more comparable and thus transparent transactions with office properties: "sometimes hard to know what the actual yield really is – for example there are few industrial transactions," and

> I think the valuation for office buildings if more transparent, and you have more information; but retail is more complex, not so many brokers have correct information; so not exactly that I try to change a valuation, but I try to give my client a correct view based on my experience and let him know if I see deviations.

A final reasoning for brokers' opinions and behavior related to property valuation for transaction purposes, gained throughout the interviews conducted, is given by the communication with in-house valuation and transaction departments. There are three real estate brokers working for large companies who exemplify the importance of the cooperation with such departments within their companies:

- "I get in touch and talk to my colleagues from the Valuation department, we look at comparable deals and who could be a potential buyer."
- "I make the contact with the appraiser, who is normally in-house, so colleague of mine. And I tell the client he should accept that valuation coming from us in-house, because we know the market; I tell him it is difficult to make the transaction at another yield. But it is not easy to manipulate the numbers, the buyer does his due diligence anyway and he finds out all details."
- "The owners come to us with higher demands, but we manage to sell – normally at a lower price; being a big company, we have a lot of information about the real estate market, so having this information advantage is easier for me. We have a very good cost controlling and project management. The colleagues know the market very well."
- "Internally, we discuss with the Investment, Valuations and Brokerage departments to settle the yield."

Figure 4.6 NVivo Word Cloud – Valuation rationale of brokers

4.4.2.2. Appraisers' opinions and behavior related to valuation

Based on the interviews conducted with real estate service providers, this work attempts to highlight the valuation rationale from the viewpoint of appraisers. A total number of 16 appraisers interviewed explain why they find valuation reports to be flexible ("value is not a fixed amount"), while exemplifying the parameters in a valuation report that can be subject to changes and thus influence the valuation outcome; by contrast, the appraisers also explain in which circumstances they cannot see a flexibility of property valuation reports.

This study also offers evidence for the pressure clients put on the appraisers and the behavior of the market actors in such circumstances.

4.4.2.2.1. APPRAISERS SEE FLEXIBILITY IN THE VALUATION REPORTS

The present research reveals that appraisers consider property valuation reports to be subject to flexibility. Of the appraisers interviewed, 12 offer extended explanations in this regard, while only 3 of them illustrate why they do not see any flexibility in valuations. All of the 12 appraisers who see flexibility in valuation reports are members of real estate organizations; moreover, one third work for large valuation and advisory corporations, while the rest of them have experience in small companies.

The advisors who see flexibility in valuations try to give their own interpretation for property valuations and appraisals: "the value is the amount a buyer is ready to pay for a property," valuation is a "necessary bad for reaching a scope," valuation is "not a static process," and it "needs to be a view into the future." The advisory role within the valuation process is also highlighted in the interviews, while pointing out that the position of the appraiser in his relationship to the client is asymmetric.

Other notable opinions related to property valuation coming from the advisors' side are comments such as "as long everything is within the legal frame,

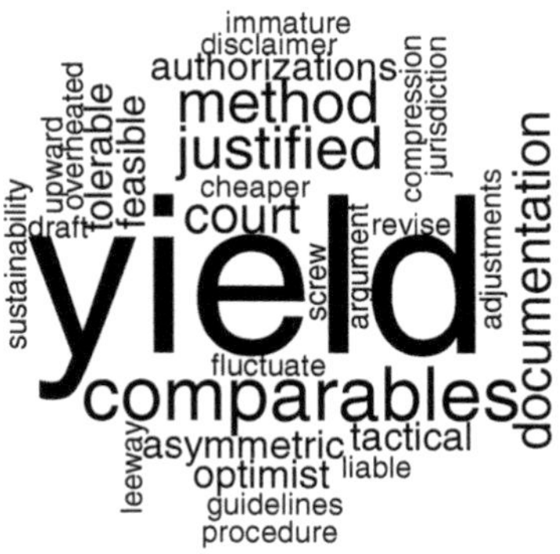

Figure 4.7 NVivo Word Cloud – Valuation rationale of appraisers

everything is possible" or "no one is interested about the actual value of the property, the interest lies in what you can do with that value once you got it, so the scope of the valuation is essential."

To summarize, the behavior of appraisers and their opinions related to the flexibility of valuation reports are based on five major argumentations related to:

- Margin of adjustability.
- Legitimate argumentation.
- Negotiation with the client.
- Particularity of the asset class.
- The fee charged by the appraiser.

The appraisers share similar opinions related to the margin of adjustability they use in the valuation reports. Some appraisers find the +/- 10% to be "normally feasible," and state that "value can fluctuate within a margin," "prices can have high dynamics," or "there is "no no-go regarding adaptations."

The appraisers who talk about the flexibility of the valuation reports and the fact that value is not a fixed amount highlight the importance of the legitimate argumentation. Appraisers find it very important to have a proper justification of the value in the valuation report they prepare. There are several analogous opinions in this sense:

- "If a property is over-rented, you make the proper documentation by explaining why you think that, and so you can lower the value."
- "Good argumentation of the market rent for example, after looking at several market reports."
- "We can be flexible, but this has to be a tolerable dimension and it has to be justifiable."
- "My standard is that I have to be able to defend my valuation opinion and have a good argumentation in a court hearing."
- "I can be flexible and adapt to clients' request regarding a valuation outcome as long as I find it justifiable."
- "The value is not so important, normally you have a logical explanation for it, given by the market and the property itself; its sustainability is important."

Another essential argument for appraisers is the negotiation with the client. An appraiser working for a small company points out that "the value is a negotiation thing, this is how I see it." His other colleagues offer exhaustive explanations for the discussions they conduct with their clients:

- "I always feel the client, I know him, and I know what he wants, so I adapt a lot."
- "I adapt myself to the market – for example, if the client wishes e.g. 2% yield but there is only 4% possible on the market, you have to meet each other in the middle."

- "The price is a comparable value, what was received in the past for a similar property; I can adapt to special requests of the client and adapt the value towards the target price, as long as I believe in that."
- "I am ready to discuss with the client and if the argument is for me correct, I am willing to be more flexible."

The flexibility of valuation reports is also given by the asset class: "a classic property has more comparable values and it is easier to valuate."

According to the opinion of another appraiser, a special asset class such as industrial real estate is more difficult to valuate, thus the flexibility margins are higher: "the demand for such properties is lower, there are few authorizations given for their operations, therefore the opinions at their valuation differ."

In other words, for a property which has more comparable transactions (such as an office building) the flexibility of the valuation report might be lower, whereas a special asset class such as industrial or logistics real estate has less comparable transactions, thus the valuation outcome might be subject to higher deviations.

Finally, an appraiser refers to the fee charged by the appraiser and connects it to the leverage some appraisers might use: "one strange thing: the cheaper an appraiser is, the better the perception about him" or "when the fee charged by the appraiser is low, he can be influenced more easily; this is very strange, but it is like that."

4.4.2.2.2. PARAMETERS THAT INFLUENCE THE VALUATION OUTCOME

The valuation outcome might vary because of several reasons enumerated by the appraisers interviewed, and these reasons can be classified into three major categories: one-time valuations, comparable transactions, and input data (yield, NOI).

A. One-time valuations

   There are appraisers who consider that a valuation report done only once can be subject to more flexibility as compared to the valuation reports done on a continuous basis, such as the mandatory yearly valuation reports for the same properties. In such cases, when the valuation is only done once, one can make use of the spread and the "margin of flexibility is higher," according to the interviewed appraisers.

B. Comparable transactions

   The comparable transactions known on the market allow a certain degree of valuation flexibility as well. An appraiser from Romania offers a detailed explanation for that:

   > You look at the transactions made in the market; it is important to have a view on them, for example the Notary Union in Romania might give such information, but this is anonymized; if you use other comparable transactions, you come to a different value.

C. Input data

The input data in a valuation outcome can be subject to most of the changes according to appraisers. In the income approach, the most used term identified with the margin of flexibility in a valuation is the yield. However, besides the yield, there is input information that can be subject to changes, such as rental income (NOI), property costs, and additional (for the valuation non-mandatory) information regarding the property.

C1. Yield (or capitalization rate)

The appraisers interviewed offer extended explanations on how the capitalization rate impacts the outcome of a valuation. In the following, some interview fragments which describe in detail the explanations appraisers give concerning the influence of input data on the valuation outcome are shown:

- "You can maneuver the cap rate very easy, this is the first thing you do, because no one understands it; no one knows how you really calculate it, or how you really came to that, or what initial income you took into account; for example you throw 7% on the paper, and its change can be justified almost always."
- "Capitalization rate is subject to negotiation."
- "The market gives this percent, and this comes from the big brokerage companies, but you have also several databases and comparable transactions."
- "If you are optimist, you estimate a higher rent and thus a higher income."
- "If we know the investors and the market well, we can make a proper yield compression."
- "The highest flexibility margin is the yield and the rent level, and from here start the discussions like 'why in Romania 8% when in Austria is only 5%?'; so there is a big pressure on the yields."
- "It does not help if you only change the yield, as said you should work at each parameter, at each input; the gross yield is interesting, you cannot explain to anybody why you used 7.5% or 8%, there is no rational explanation; but this is why it is also very easy to find out if someone worked and tried to change only the gross yield."

C2. Net operating income and property costs

The NOI has a high impact, according to the appraisers. The most relevant factors that influence the valuation outcome can be summarized into the following categories:

- Tenant lists.
- Service charges.
- Management and maintenance costs.

Figure 4.8 NVivo Word Cloud – Appraisers' flexibility in valuations

- Refurbishment costs.
- Other assumptions:
  - Technical assumptions.
  - Operating restrictions.
  - Expected use life.

D. Miscellaneous

- "Problems with a neighbor shouldn't be disclosed or taken into account; for tactical reasons there might be that one or the other information in this direction might not be disclosed."

To conclude, an experienced appraiser explains that

> it does not help if you only change the yield, you should work at each parameter, at each input . . . my disclaimer is you should use this "screw" in adapting all parameters of your valuation report – such as rental income (e.g. to be adapted according to the floor), service charges (to be positioned in a correct manner, otherwise you can notice the differences), yield.

Additionally, another appraiser indicates that "in the adaptation of the value there are no limits; I experienced cases when I had a devaluation of 30–50%, depending on the property and its problems."

4.4.2.2.3. APPRAISERS SEE NO FLEXIBILITY IN VALUATION REPORTS

Three of the 16 appraisers interviewed explain their reasons for not being able to be flexible when preparing a valuation report. They have experience with all three asset classes and work in small, medium-sized, and large companies.

An appraiser notes that for him "a difference of +/- 10% is big; I am generally not flexible." The reasons why appraisers do not see flexibility in valuation reports can be divided into:

- Image and reliability: "My image and the authority that I received to sign a valuation report are very important. I do not want to lose that of course," "It is very important that this margin is not overrun because it is not reliable any more," and "I have to defend the valuation report from three perspectives – mathematically, scientifically and according to the market."
- Asset class – (mainly) office buildings: "For an office building, newly built, prime location, the margin of flexibility is lower than for industrial premises, located in a suburban area in Vienna. Here the margin of flexibility is higher . . . another example, for office towers in Vienna: you have let's say a yield of 4–4.25%. But for a piece of land, since the sale price might be something between 119 and 400 Euro per sqm, the yield differs much more and of course the value computed differs within a higher margin," and "I give arguments which are concrete and based on comparable transactions."
- Reports for the same property: "If you make reports for the same property over the years you have to be stricter, you must not make use of the margins," and "more difficult or impossible to correct or to cover up the mistakes you made in the past valuations."

4.4.2.2.4. PRESSURE PUT ON APPRAISERS

The last sub-section presents the importance of the yield for the valuation outcome and the fact that it can be subject to most of the changes in a valuation, according to the opinions of the interviewed appraisers.

In addition to that, another appraiser points out that "the highest flexibility margin is the yield and the rent level," and from here the discussions concerning the pressure put on the yields starts. The pressure on the yields is basically given by the pressure companies have concerning the valuation outcome.

Eight appraisers working for small, medium-sized, and large companies with experience in commercial real estate (logistics, office, retail properties) explain their opinions for the pressure their clients have:

- "The big companies do not have a wish to have a big upward valuation trend. This is their interest, and this is what they tell the appraisers; there are clients that expect a certain value; when a property is disposed, also here there are special expectations."
- "Valuations are not ordered to find out the value, but to reach a target."
- "Besides the pressure they put on regarding the value expected, they do not want to pay you so much money."

The interviewed appraisers share rather identical opinions when it comes to the pressure their clients exercise regarding the valuation outcome. On one hand, this pressure is explained by property financing, through statements such as

> a client wanted full financing from a bank; he wanted a valuation around 30% over the market value, so that he could receive more money from the bank; the clients try to convince you to do that, but I do not accept,

or

> it happens very often that clients come to me and tell me the exact value to be reached, because of the financing situation, I would say that the clients generally try to bring the market value in the direction they are interested in,

or "there might be that a client has financing on that certain property, but he tells me I should make the valuation without taking this into account," or "the clients have phantasies which we cannot accomplish sometimes; there is a lot of conflict potential here, between us, the financing bank and the requirements and expectations of our clients."

Appraisers also mention that they had to decline mandates because they did not want to, or they were not able to, meet the expectations of their clients. As one appraiser discloses, "the investor (the client) always has his own expectation about what value should be reached," and it "happened several times that I had to decline mandates because the clients wanted to have a higher value than I could deliver."

Finally, another appraiser working for a medium-sized company notes that the pressure exercised on appraisers might rise as soon the interests rise again:

> The risk is that the projects, especially the construction projects, will become more expensive due to a higher financing amount and thus the clients will expect even higher values. I expect the pressure put on the appraisers from clients' side will rise, because they will expect a higher endowment. Hopefully the interest rates will remain stable in the next years.

4.4.2.3. *Clients' opinions and behavior related to valuation*

4.4.2.3.1. STATEMENTS FROM THE CLIENTS' PERSPECTIVES

The following part of the research aims to reveal and document the value drivers and the opinions investors have towards commercial property valuation for transaction purposes. Seven clients working (or having worked for) big, institutional companies within an international environment offer their generic insights on commercial property valuation and explanations what the valuation reports are needed for, according to their opinion and expertise.

Among general remarks concerning property valuation, coming from the clients' side who act as medium-sized and big institutional investors in the commercial real estate markets, the following statements can be distinguished: "valuations are for us important because of the business model we follow; we have to rely on values in order to conduct our business properly," "in transactions, a valuation report is necessary for an investor in order to base himself on a specific number; so he wants a number, not an opinion or a clarification," or

> I do not send all the information to the appraisers, I filter it depending on what they need; for example, we are not allowed to disclose to them the CapEx [capital expenditure; investments] we planned; and it has to be agreed with your superior, what exactly you send to the appraiser.

Moving on, three other important players with institutional background explain their interest to keep the value of the property stable throughout the transaction process until the property is sold:

- "The best case is when the value remains stable throughout the whole sale process and it should not get higher, otherwise the disposal is not a success anymore; when the fair value gets higher, the sale success is lower; it does not matter, fair value or book value, after the disposal the fair value is introduced in the balance sheet."
- "When we sell, the price has to be higher than the valuation amount."
- "The target is that the value remains constant; when you change the appraiser, given the same market environment, and you assign another appraiser, you come to different values."

Furthermore, while another client from a large company points out that it is important to sell above the book value, the interests for property valuation at disposal are opposite – during the property acquisition process, the valuation needs to be higher than the acquisition price. This reasoning is described by clients who work for medium-sized and big companies:

- "When buying a property, I try to find a way to raise the valuation to an amount higher than the acquisition price; if the price is lower than the fair value at the acquisition point, I have no interest in buying the property; on the other hand, the fair value should not be too low because of the financing (the computation of the loan to value)."
- "Valuation is very important, especially the valuation done at the acquisition point; lots of acquisitions did not take place because of that; for example, the price is 25 M Euro but the valuation is only 24.5 M, this is a no-go for us; the value has to be higher than what I pay, otherwise I do not do the deal; this is why it is important to understand the valuation and the numbers and computations behind; the rule is: the valuation must not be below the acquisition price and we have to look at the development of the asset in the next 8–10 years."

Finally, three other clients (each of them working for a small, medium-sized and a large company) refer to the importance they give to property valuations and to their need to have either a valuation department in-house or at least internally double-check the valuation reports for the properties they have interest in:

- "We do our valuations on a quarterly basis and we also have our internal valuation team because it is important for us to have our own opinion on the assets valued; we use the external appraisers for the funds we need to valuate."
- "We have to be involved, to know the yields and the replacement costs for example, or the construction price and of course the values; we interact with the appraisers, especially with our internal valuation team, in order to have the best market knowledge."
- "We then internally price up the details of all the information we get about transactions."
- "But we also have our own appraisers, for internal audit purposes."
- "I am an expert in this field and do my own calculations anyway."

4.4.2.3.2. CLIENTS SEE FLEXIBILITY IN VALUATION REPORTS

The previous chapter presented a qualitative perspective on the opinions of the appraisers on the valuation process, explaining the reasoning why they find valuation reports to be subject to changes, and thus subject to flexibility. Eight clients present their viewpoints on the flexibility they see in the valuation reports. Among them, 6 are not members of a real estate organization, half of them work for public companies, and the other half for non-public companies.

On one hand, the clients seek direct communication with their appraiser in order to explain and talk about the valuation expectations, and there are notable explanations disclosed in this regard:

- "I have always told the appraiser I worked with what my expectations are, because I wanted to avoid surprises regarding the specific valuation."
- "I have to explain him [to the appraiser] the property and its problems; depending on the direction I want to follow, I clarify with him a certain plus in the valuation; but I have to stay realistic, if the property does not function so good, if the rental income is not as expected, I define with the appraiser a realistic devaluation."
- "When I sell a property, I have to sell it over the fair value; it is a must: either the sale price is higher than the fair value, or the transaction is on hold; in this case I am indeed in contact with my appraiser; I discuss with him the cap rates and the possibilities to adjust them in order to reach a next fair value which is lower, to be able to sell that property; so it's all about offer and demand, the appraiser receives all information within a data room and everyone does his work; so my appraiser receives all information, I try to be

transparent; but I also explain the specific fair value or the price it is wanted to be reached."

On the other hand, the clients give several arguments about the parameters they consider to be subject to changes (subject to flexibility) within valuation reports, and highlight their interest for having a certain degree of flexibility: "I search for a specific value because I need it; no one wants to hear the opinion of the appraiser, maybe only the banks," and "there are nuances, depending on whether you want to sell or to buy; I can use arguments both when I want to have a rent level of 18 €/sqm or of 16."

The following part of the study will exemplify the concrete parameters that the clients consider to be subject to flexibility in a valuation report.

4.4.2.3.3. PARAMETERS THAT INFLUENCE THE VALUATION OUTCOME

The clients specify three main components of a commercial property valuation that can be – in their view – subject to changes: the yield (or capitalization rate), the investments in the property (capital expenditure), and the rental income.

Clients expect that the appraiser has enough market knowledge to "come to a proper capitalization rate" and point out that it is important to discuss it with the appraisal:

> with the yield you have the biggest flexibility, I find it ok to discuss it with the appraiser; it is not ok not to have an opinion; you explain your arguments, you have a technical and specialist discussion with him and this should be acceptable.

The second parameter is related to the impact investments have on the outcome of a property valuation. Due to this fact, there are clients who mention that such information is sometimes kept aside and not fully disclosed to the responsible appraiser. There are even cases when the company's board or other bodies within a company may give instructions for not announcing certain planned investments: "we even have an internal request not to send them all investments we planned, in order to avoid a change of the value downwards because of the planned cost increases."

The clients are aware that appraisers are flexible when it comes to forecasting the capital expenditure and explain it may happen

> that the next owner does not want to invest so much in a property, therefore we do not want to tell him that a special investment as CapEx is planned; these are things which the potential buyer should find out by himself when he is doing the Due Diligence.

A last important component is the rental income, with a highlight on retail properties due to the additional income given by turnover rents (a percentage

Figure 4.9 NVivo Word Cloud – Clients' flexibility in valuations

of the retail tenant's turnover throughout a certain period) or specialty leasing income (islands, short-term leasing, etc.), which are mostly common for shopping centers:

- "In retail, the valuations are more complex I think, and the values are prone to change more drastically than in the case of the other assets; what it is sometimes forgotten here and it surely makes a difference are the turnover rents, they are above the contractual rents, if the tenants reach a certain turnover."
- "There is always a discussion on the specialty leasing income – that additional income which comes from the short-term leasing as promotions, islands in the shopping center or in the parking place and so on."

To conclude, clients consider that the rental income is an important factor subject to flexibility and it can change if one "presents it more optimistic."

4.4.2.3.4. CLIENTS SEE NO FLEXIBILITY IN VALUATION REPORTS

Among the 26 clients interviewed, 2 of them express their reasons why they cannot be flexible with the mandatory valuation reports prepared for their commercial real estate portfolios.

The first opinion comes from a senior representative of an investment company who manages commercial real estate portfolios within the CEE region. He explains that the valuation reports cannot be subject to changes or have a certain level of flexibility as long they are done on a continuous basis for the same investor:

> you have a fund from Germany investing in CEE – they require a valuation each year; you cannot cheat the numbers so easily, since the valuation is done so often; this is why there are no big differences in the valuation here, of course there can be deviations; so you pretty much know what a property used to be.

On the other hand, another representative of a large investor argues that the mandated valuation teams are not flexible when it comes to institutional investors and the discussions regarding such valuations are normally conducted by the company's management board: "hard co-operation and relationship with the appraisers; they are normally not flexible, especially in my case when they work for institutional investors; there are always negotiations with them, and these negotiations are normally solved on Board level."

4.4.2.3.5. CONTACT BETWEEN VALUATION REPORTS

Throughout the interviews, the clients have been asked what their behavior with their appraisers is, whether they keep in contact on a continuous basis or whether their contact with the appraiser only takes place when the property valuation report is needed. Twelve of the clients exemplified the cases in which they seek contact with their mandated appraiser. All of them work for small, medium-sized, and large companies.

However, it can be distinguished that 3 of the clients who mention that contact with their appraisers is made on a continuous basis come from the field of logistics real estate and other 3 of the 12 clients have experience with both logistics and office real estate properties.

Several reasons can be identified for the need of continuous contact with the appraisers: for transaction purposes, during the property development or construction phase, because of the banks' requirements or needed financing, or for information reasons, in order to be up to date with the market evolution.

The clients in charge of property development projects explain that the contact with the appraiser is needed, as the construction project is subject to continuous changes: "in development is different, if a project suffered massive changes – like the project timeline for example – I have to update the valuation report," "I need to stay in constant contact with the appraiser, in order to observe what possibilities he has regarding the further development of the property; in the next development stages, the next valuation will be needed," "have to conduct a special construction survey," and "we do valuation on potential land banks, so we need to provide the appraiser with lots of information."

The following reasons (financial purposes, during transactions) why the contact with the appraiser takes place between valuations are complementary:

- "When a valuation needs to be done before an acquisition, then I have contact with the appraisers also during these six months period between the valuations."
- "Inter-group transactions or at the request of the banks."
- "I need to get more capital from the bank throughout the project – when purchasing a property, there are costs for the zoning and we make pre-calculations of the construction costs; in this stage we need the bank financing, thus the valuation report."

- "For financing reasons, if the bank requires that for its balance sheet; in this regard it is important to be aware that you should be also ready for a devaluation if it is required; if you cannot do that than your business is generally not going so well."

Finally, there are clients who want to maintain an active contact with their appraisers thought the year, also between the needed valuation reports, pointing out the importance of possessing the latest market knowledge:

- "We also follow other properties in the market."
- "Have to be always involved, to know the yields and the replacement costs."
- "I update the appraiser in order to keep track with the specific asset and with the market in general; I forward him market information, market reports and so on."
- "We want to have the confirmation that we have sustainable values, but we also confirm to them what contracts will soon expire, we discuss whether the rent is sustainable; all of that needs consultation and explanations."
- "Frequent contact with each other; we provide them updates on what has been changed and other info like permits or income."

Additionally, a client highlights the involvement and the continuous contact with the appraisers throughout the year because of the mandatory internal audit: "part of the audit process, we have auditors coming in, discuss, check, this is why the value is very important."

By contrast, most of the clients interviewed (19 out of 26) claim that there is no need for an additional contact with the appraisal throughout the interval between property valuation reports. Hence, there is a heterogeneous group of respondents assessing that there is no need to have contact with the appraiser between valuation reports. The clients have senior-level experience throughout the entire investigated region, with a background in public and non-public companies, and manage all three commercial real estate asset classes (retail, office logistics).

The clients indicate there is neither a "need" nor an "interest" to contact the appraiser between valuation reports, and explain that such contact is event driven: "for standing investments I would say it is not necessary to give updates to your appraiser, this applies only for development projects," "we generally need only a one time valuation, only at a special reference date," "I only have contact when a valuation is needed, in the past years when I worked for a big listed company, this happened 4 times a year, so this is more than enough," and "appraisers need to have basic information, it does not make sense to have a repeated contact with them; only when you need the valuation you get in contact with them."

Sharing information with the appraiser between valuation reports seems to be a critical topic for the most part of the clients: "I do not want to disclose him any information in-between; we definitely avoid to share information with the appraiser between transactions if this is not requested by third parties," "I do not give the appraiser any information between the valuations, he should do that on his own the next time he makes the report," "this might only create confusion," "it is a matter of confidentiality," "otherwise he has more information than he needs, and this could be shared with other parties," and "I have no need or no interest to give him any other updates or information besides what he needs once a year."

Besides the main concern of information disclosure, a client mentions that throughout the period between the necessary valuation reports the situation with a certain property might change, so the "work load can be bigger."

A memorable statement about the contact as well as the information exchange with the appraiser in the period of time between valuation reports comes from a client who explains: "Theoretically speaking it would be good to have a continuous process and relationship, it is nice to have. But in practice this is not done." Finally, the qualitative analysis with NVivo shows that the investors from non-public companies tend to not have continuous contact with the appraisers, between the (yearly) valuations.

4.4.2.4. *Other market actors who play a role in the valuation process*

The present research from the interviews conducted reveals that there may be additional market actors who might play a role in commercial property valuation for transaction purposes. In this sense, the interview partners highlight the role the financial institutions play when deciding upon assigning a valuation mandate. "It always depends on the bank," as one small investor with experience in logistics real estate points out.

Among the 52 interviewed market actors, 14 of them provide similar representations of the bank's role in the valuation process – 8 of them are clients (most of them working for small companies) and the other 6 are advisors (most of them appraisers, working for large companies).

The clients have analogous opinions when it comes to explaining the role banks play for the valuation of a property that needs financing. While some investors are more cautious in their relationship with the bank ("I am transparent when dealing with the bank; I have a product to finance and I think it would be a big problem if I would try to make the values nicer for the bank"), others indicate that the banks have an active participation when deciding upon assigning a mandate to a specific appraiser:

- "There are times when you have to work with another one [appraiser] because the financing bank requires that."
- "Normally we work with the same appraiser, if it is not that we need a valuation for the bank."
- "No one actually wants to hear the opinion of the appraiser, maybe only the banks."
- "Important that the appraiser comes from a big, renowned company; he should have the big brand behind him and know the local market; this is the

perfect situation, especially in my case, when you work in an institutional environment and have a bank behind, you want your appraiser to be reliable, to have a brand and a track-record."

A last notable observation that comes from a client having a background in an institutional environment, but also in a medium-sized company, is the formality or confirmation character of the valuation reports: "three steps process: first, I have my expectations, second, the appraiser verifies them, third, the bank confirms," "valuation is a formality needed by the bank and this is why I normally need a formal report and a third opinion," and

> the appraiser is only the first step of verification; the bank is important because we need its financing capital, besides the equity; the equity should be as little as possible and our target is to get as much external finance as we can; since this depends on the bank, the appraiser is only a vehicle to reach the target we expect.

This last remark is confirmed by an appraiser, working for a small company, who said: "we check the valuations we do for the banks, we discuss with the bank's clients and it is always like that – everyone wants to show a higher equity through a higher value of the property."

The advisors further emphasize the role banks play in commercial property valuation. From a particular point of view of an international broker, the feedback from the bank is sometimes more important than the feedback of clients. In his opinion, the credibility of the brokers on the real estate market might be put into question when the broker does not estimate an adequate yield in line with the expectations of the financing bank:

> And not only the feedback of the client counts, also does the feedback of the bank. For example, you make a valuation for an industrial client for financing purposes; if the bank estimates a yield of 8% but my company calculated 7%, there is a high probability that the bank does not recommend me for further transactions, they would say the investor should go to my competitors. I would say the banks have a lot to say in this regard, of what they expect. So losing the trust on the market costs me more than losing a fee from a client.

Finally, an appraiser with leading corporate experience reiterates the relevance of the company's brand for the valuation reports. He explains that financing banks expect valuation reports conducted by renowned brokerage, advisory, and valuation companies:

> there are corporate clients that need that brand, for third parties [e.g. banks]; this is the single motive why valuations from big companies are ordered;

Figure 4.10 NVivo Word Cloud – Other parties in commercial property valuation

> otherwise the client would want the cheapest appraiser, since he does not want to spend so much money on such stuff, and because an appraiser who asks for a lower fee can be influenced more easily.

4.4.2.5. Preliminary conclusions related to the valuation rationale

The research conducted addresses the theoretical frame of Behavioral Real Estate, with its specific issues such as availability heuristic, confirmation bias, smoothing and lagging, as well as client's feedback. These findings are consistent with previous ones that have established that "there is a large discrepancy between the prescriptive, normative valuation process and the descriptive, positive process, which is cognitively biased and subject to agency problems" (Salzman & Zwinkels 2017: 92).

The results from the in-depth interviews related to valuation rationale demonstrate that the valuation task is often reduced to the specific motives of the market actors.

First, the real estate brokers emphasize that valuations are subjective and try to convince their clients to accept a certain value (transaction price) and explain that they refuse mandates when the discrepancy between the clients' expectations and their own opinion (taking in to account the time they would have to invest for the commercialization of the property) is too high.

Furthermore, real estate brokers working for large agencies make use of the information coming from other in-house departments, such as Valuation and Investment. In this case, the so-called Chinese walls within such service companies can be challenged.

Second, the appraisers also find valuation outcomes to be subject to flexibility to a certain extend. The most important parameters that might influence the valuation are the following: one-time valuations, comparable transactions, input data including NOI and property costs, and the yield. While most of the interviewed appraisers consider a 10% deviation acceptable, there are also opinions that the valuation reports cannot suffer high deviations due to qualitative considerations (e.g., own image or reliability) as well as asset class (office buildings or properties with a high number of comparable transactions).

The results also show that client pressure or client feedback plays a significant part in property valuation. Specifically, the appraisers illustrate that the main pressure is put on the yield, with the property financing and the banks' requirements in the background. Moreover, appraisers explain that discussing the valuation outcome is mostly subject to a negotiation technique and in extreme cases, when the clients' expectations are too high, the appraisers find themselves in the position of declining mandates.

Third, the clients offer solid documentation of their interests for having a stable property value throughout the transaction process, until the property is sold. By contrast, when a property is in acquisition, the aim is to raise the valuation to an amount higher than the acquisition price. Moreover, clients point out the need to sell above the book value and they express the concern that when appraisers change, the values change as well.

As for contact with the appraisers between valuations, the clients highlight the need for having continuous contact, mostly in the following cases: during the construction phase; due to the banks' requirements, because of the internal audit; or to have market updates. However, the clients interviewed claim that there is no need for a contact between valuation reports due to information disclosure risks and property changes which might lead to a higher work load for both parties.

Finally, the study led to the conclusion that among the two main categories of market actors (clients and service providers), there is a third category which plays a significant role for commercial property valuations: the financing banks. They are active participants when it comes to deciding upon assigning an appraiser and prefer valuation reports from well-established appraisers or real estate service firms (agencies).

4.4.3. *Anchors in valuation*

As Salzman and Zwinkels (2017: 90) explain, anchoring is the most described source of biased valuations, by causing valuation outcomes to be biased "towards an initial starting estimate." This bias is even stronger when the appraiser is not comfortable with the property or with the real estate environment, or is unfamiliar with the specific real estate market.

The result of the interviews with experienced appraisers in the investigated region aims to identify consistent findings for this significant pillar of Behavioral Real Estate – valuation anchoring. The appraisers were asked to explain in which cases they tend to build-up a valuation report based on previous assumptions of other appraiser colleagues and whether such "anchors" have an impact on their judgment and valuation.

Seven qualified appraisers indicate that they look through precedent valuation reports; all of them have experience in preparing valuation reports for the three asset classes and come from small (4), medium-sized (1), and large companies (2).

There are appraisers explaining that they "always look at past valuations if available"; one appraiser, who works for a large advisory and brokerage company, and whose clients are large, institutional real estate companies, even admits that, in his company, "we definitely take the previous reports in consideration, this is basically the starting point; we never start at zero." Nevertheless, an appraiser who also works for a large company has the disclaimer that such information on previous valuation reports might not be available: "I would like to know the former price or value increases but such info is not easy to get."

The target for obtaining the former valuation reports is certainly "to know the past values" in order "to move around this amount," as one appraiser working at a medium-sized company mentions. He also adds that knowing the result is very important "because I can do a good estimation with that; if I came to a big difference (10–20%) between my value and the past one I received from the client, I ask the client why this can be." In addition to that, the appraisers explain that assumptions such as expected use life and especially capitalization are important milestones for a better assessment of the already-conducted valuation reports.

The main reason for using such anchors in valuation uttered by the appraisers is given by the lack of experience, either on a certain real estate market or with the valuated property:

- "When I have to make a valuation for a property or in a country I do not know so well, I always do my own valuation and then look and compare mine to the former ones; afterwards I can make changes, if I consider they are relevant; it is important to talk to the other appraisers and look for advice, in order to get a complete view of the market situation."
- "Outside Austria we always work with local appraisers, you cannot do without them, because they know the market very good; of course, we look at the former valuation reports and check the assumptions."

The fact that the previous valuation reports are treated as guidelines for the current valuation is articulated by appraisers who work for small companies in Austria and need to conduct valuations within the CEE region:

- "I take indeed other past valuations as guideline and I want to stay within these lines; in such a way there are no questions regarding what I deliver."
- "We check the validity of the assumptions and if they are still correct, we adapt our valuation in an appropriate manner."

To conclude, an appraiser working for a small company stresses the inflexibility when he identifies past valuation reports:

> "When I know there have been also other valuation reports made for the same property, I am really inflexible."

4.4.4. The relationship between clients and advisors

4.4.4.1. Distinctions advisors make between clients

The next section of the study aims to identify evidence on specific characteristics of behavior that advisors have towards their clients, what kind of distinctions they make – if any – and how these can be classified. The qualitative interviews conducted with 28 advisors (brokers and appraisers with senior-level experience) indicate consistent differences in behavior towards clients, whereas the reasoning is similar and there can be differentiations by company size and long-term partnership with clients.

Nonetheless, the appraisers, especially, indicate differences they make in their behavior towards clients, and these are linked to the cultural background, real estate expertise, expectations of the clients, personal relationship with the clients, and valuation purpose.

Among the 28 service providers, an impressive number (19) illustrate in detail that they differentiate between the partnership with specific clients depending on company size; moreover, most of the interviewed clients (22) explain that the difference in their behavior is even deeper if they have a repeated business relationship with their clients and not an event-driven mandate. Notable evidence is the fact that most of the advisors that refer to these differences are appraisers.

When deciding upon cooperation with small companies, the brokers – especially those working for large, international companies – highlight the importance of the screening they need to conduct before accepting a certain mandate:

- "We do a client screening right at the beginning; since the business is uncertain, it is very important to choose your transactions carefully."
- "We check the track record."

Furthermore, the brokers interviewed explain that they prefer to work with clients from big corporations, whereas financial situation and trust seem to be the most significant argumentations:

- "You establish strict rules for the smaller ones, because you do not know their financial situation; check his credit worthiness . . . financing is important and whether the company has legal issues, this is a negative sign."
- "With the big ones, who are well-known, I do not need any contracts or written agreements, a mail is enough to settle up the fee; this is normal on the market, but with the small companies I need a contract, to define our partnership in a more detailed way."
- "Trust is also important, I behave differently to my customers when they are well established on the market and when they come from big companies."

At the same time, a broker working at a large, international brokerage and advisory company highlights the tension that might come from clients from large companies: "I feel a certain pressure depending on the size of the company – the big ones put more pressure on you and you have to deliver more quickly and to adapt more."

A similar detriment is assessed by a real estate broker who works for a small company and points to the fact that the smaller companies have fewer decision-making procedures:

- "The small ones are maybe more important for me because they are faster, their decision process is fast and that is much better for me because I come to my mandates."
- "Big names help you get other bigger names, but the certainty comes from the smaller ones."

When differentiating between clients coming from small or large companies, the arguments given by the appraisers are numerous. Still, what can be identified as similar is the adverse approach of two appraisers working at small companies in Austria and Romania towards clients from large companies: "big companies are complicated, the process always takes longer" and "the big ones are more time consuming, and they need more extensive reports."

However, the majority of the appraisers indeed make a difference by company size and tend to favor the clients coming from large companies; "big client, well established on the market . . . I treat him slightly different," "when I deal with the big companies I have no fear and no worries," "this is why I might be more flexible when it comes to a bigger company I have as client," and "we prefer to deal with bigger companies, with larger portfolios because it is much easier to deal with – the valuation assumptions are similar, the communication is only with one party, it is easier to handle."

Appraisers give further arguments for why they tend to work with big companies rather than with small ones, given by the following annotated advantages:

- *Information*: "with the big ones I normally have framework agreements for our cooperation; the advantage for that is that I receive information which is not made public on the market" and "the important clients are the big ones, long-term, and I know them and what they need."
- *Professionalism and data quality*: "big ones are more professional, with those new on the market you have to spend more time and have to go more into detail," "big companies are much more flexible and the data quality is much better," "difficult sometimes to work with a small client, a private one, because it is very hard to get from him all the information that you need for your valuation; this is why I am more cautious in such cases," and "big companies have accurate data and it is easy to work with the long-term partners because you already have the documents needed."
- *Financial benefits*: "I am aware the big companies work with higher budgets so I adapt my request about the fee also to that," "if the client operates on losses, he loses his credibility in front of me," "I make a difference in the price, the

more mandates I get, the better the price," "price differences but only if I receive more orders from the same client, so it is about the quantity; if there is a company with a larger portfolio and a well-known brand, than I give discounts, otherwise I stick to the price if there is only one property in Romania for example," and "for the small clients I normally have fixed prices."
- *Continuity*: "the big ones come back, I have an ongoing cooperation with them, but the small ones usually do not."

Only 3 brokers and/or appraisers among the 28 advisors interviewed (2 advisors work at small companies, one works at a large one) do not assert any difference in their behavior towards clients, as a broker from a large advisory and brokerage company notes: "I do not make any difference between them . . . you have to adapt."

Apart from company size, the advisors highlight the distinction they make by the periodicity of the mandates received. Thus, most of the advisors interviewed explain why they prefer having a long-term business relationship with their clients, hence preferring working on a continuous basis rather than accepting mandates as a one-time event. Furthermore, the advisors interviewed also illustrate their behavior towards new clients.

The brokers who participated in this research emphasize the "difference between the scope of the mandate and extend," mentioning that they prefer working for a client on a continuous basis; in this way, "the work load is bigger, but so is the focus."

When differentiating between the long-term clients versus new ones, both brokers and appraisers express their cautiousness towards their behavior with the clients they hadn't known before. They highlight that the investigation of the credit worthiness of potential clients plays a major role. Some of the noteworthy explanations given by advisors can be illustrated as follows:

- "You establish strict rules for the unknown ones."
- "When I deal with a new client, I am very cautious; I check where the money comes from and I check if he is serious."

Figure 4.11 NVivo Word Cloud – Appraisers make a difference between clients

- "If I represent the buyer, I look at the company, the value of the assets, the history; if I deal with a potential buyer, I check his credit worthiness; also, the financing is important and whether he the company has legal issues, this could be a negative sign."
- "Since the business is uncertain, it is very important to choose your transactions carefully; if I have a no-name client, I am much more circumspect, I always check the track-record."
- "If I deal with someone new on the market . . . I am very cautious."
- "When dealing with new clients I do not know, I am always more careful; I pay attention to the documents I send, because of the liability risk; I am liable for what I send and what I say, this is why I am so cautious; but when I already know the client, I have of course much more confidence."

The appraisers are those who tend to differentiate more between clients, as opposed to the real estate brokers. They also give extended argumentations to justify why they are inclined to favor the business relationships with long-term clients. Their interests for a long-term partnership with their clients are reflected by the following remarks:

- "Main interest is the partnership and that we have a long-term business relationship with a client."
- "Recurring clients: I try to establish a good contact with them, to adapt to their needs, in order to make them happy and trust me for future valuations; this is why I really try to adapt to their needs."
- "The long-term partnership is also important, but this unfolds automatically if the relationship is on a trustworthy basis; if my client is satisfied with my work, he assigns me for future mandates as well."
- "The client's satisfaction is the most important thing for me, in this way I know that he comes back."

Additionally, the appraisers assert a higher leverage for continuous property valuation mandates and thus long-term partnership with the clients, and these motivations are divided into:

- *Transparency and trust*: "it is important to know the client, the better I know him, the more transparent I am," "as appraiser I am always open to my client and there has to be a relationship based on trust," and "I have long term business partnerships with some clients, most of them are real estate funds which need periodical valuation reports; with them I also conclude frame agreements, when we set the price and the timelines."
- *Flexibility*: "the longer I know my client, the more flexible I am."
- *Service-orientation towards long-term clients*: "if an old client tells us he needs a valuation within two weeks for example, so if it has to be done very fast, we do that; but if I deal with a new client and he tells me the same, I do not make the valuation so fast, I tell him I need more time," "on the long term

I work differently with my clients, it is not a linear process or relationship; when I have a big work load, I choose that client with whom I worked more together," and "if the probability for a long-term partnership is higher, I am also more flexible."

- *Lower fees and premiums*: "when dealing with long-term partners I give more discounts of course," "the recurring clients are important and I am ready to negotiate a fee lower than 3% for a transaction, knowing that I work with a long-term partner," "big companies work with big volumes and on the long-term, which is better for us, although they make more pressure to go lower with the price, there is also a bigger margin," and "I am open and ready to accept a lower fee if I consider it will be a long-lasting business relationship."
- *Data quality*: "in case of the one-time clients, there are a lot of problems with the data quality; it is hard to receive the complete lease agreements, the plans, you have to make the research on your own, you have to make more assumptions and have more disclaimers, so it is very difficult and time-consuming; it is therefore more comfortable to work with bigger clients, for whom you do several valuations over a period of time."
- *Access to market data*: "we prefer to have the long-term partnerships because we have more available information" and "frame agreements with the clients we work on a constant basis and this is an advantage because in this way we come to more comparable values and we have much more documentation possibilities."

Nonetheless, two real estate brokers note that one should be loyal to the client that pays the fee and adapt to each client: "I do not make any difference between them . . . you have to adapt" and "I am loyal towards the client who pays me."

The result of the study shows that the differences in advisors' behavior towards clients are not only due to the company size and long-term partnership, they can also depend on cultural background, real estate expertise, expectations of the clients, personal relationship with the clients, and valuation purpose.

Two real estate brokers indicate that they note the difference depending on the volume of "research parameters" as well as "between real estate specialists – those who work in real estate companies – and non-property companies," whereas the second category of clients "require more assistance and more work load."

From the 16 interviewed appraisers, 11 of them illustrate their motives for the differences they make in their behavior towards clients. Most of the appraisers who disclose other differences they make in their behavior towards clients have experience in commercial real estate and work at large, medium-sized, and small companies.

Like the opinions of the real estate brokers, the appraisers' behavior towards clients may also depend on the real estate expertise or company background of their clients:

- "I change my behavior depending on how much I know that the client knows."
- "When I work with international investors who know the market or know the real estate business, when they are more experienced, it is very easy."

- "There is a big difference when working with clients; there are those who know the market and make the research on their own, and there are those who ask a lot of questions because they are not into so much details."
- "It is all about whether the client know the business or no."

Moreover, the relationship with the clients plays a significant role and the appraisers claim they behave "really different, depending on the client and on the mandate: clients are very different, so it depends also on them and on their strategy with the property," "different decision-makers in big companies and I have to take care from whom I receive the mandate for a devaluation from," "depending on the communication I have with the specific client," and "important to know what the client wants and what we give."

Other factors for drawing a distinction in their behavior with clients are the cultural background ("cultural problems, then I have another approach") and the expectations of the clients ("the perspective is very subjective, and the clients have different expectations; you also have the human side, with wishes and expectations").

A final distinction set forth by appraisers is given by the valuation purpose, and they annotate that their behavior and the relationship towards clients can vary because of that:

- "it always depends on the valuation scope."
- "sometimes the clients do not tell us or partly tell us what the scope really is."
- "several reasons for the valuation – you want to know the value, or you want to confirm it."
- "receive a mandate by an arbitrator or you can receive a mandate from a third party for a second or third opinion."
- "the valuation is made for different purposes, either for the bank or for tax purposes; therefore, the relationship with the investor is also different."

In addition to the differences identified in the behavior of real estate brokers and appraisers, there is one appraiser working for an international agency who points out his awareness that the clients have their own differences in behavior and act based on certain interests. According to his experience, the company's brand of the appraiser has the most significance for international or institutional clients:

> The brand – there are corporate clients that need that brand, for third parties. This is the single motive why valuations are ordered from large companies. Otherwise the client would want the cheapest appraiser, since he does not want to spend so much money on such stuff, and because a cheap appraiser can be influenced more easily.

On a final note, the outcome of the interviews conducted with 28 advisors exhibits that some of the real estate brokers (6), appraisers (2), and brokers and appraisers (2) make note of the impartiality of their behavior towards clients. Half of these advisors are members of real estate organizations.

In this respect, the real estate brokers with an international background explain that all clients are important, and they are treated in the "same professional manner," thus "you have to adapt to each of them" and "fulfill everyone's expectations regarding the quality of your work, the information and the work style."

From the appraisers' side, there are a few acknowledgements that a transparent relationship with the clients is aimed at, and no difference in behavior is made: "I always work based on confidentiality and trust, this is the most important point," as one appraiser working at a small company discloses. Finally, another appraiser also working at a small company concludes:

> I act very realistic to these wishes from my clients, my feedback is based on clear numbers. It also depends on the clients I deal with. For example, the bigger companies, especially the banks, budget the devaluations.

4.4.4.2. Long-term partnership between clients and appraisers

One of the outcomes of the interviews with the advisors unfolds the fact that especially the appraisers highlight the advantages of a long-term business partnership with their clients, who mandate them for property valuation reports throughout the years.

Likewise, the clients also emphasize their aim for a continuous and durable partnership with the appraisers that valuate their real estate portfolios. Among the 24 clients interviewed, the majority of them (21) explain their motives for mandating the same appraiser throughout a longer period of time, while disclosing the importance they give to personal contact with their appraisal.

The clients who note that they strive for long-term cooperation with appraisers have expertise with all commercial real estate asset classes – still, with a notable focus on logistics real estate – and work in small, medium-sized, or large companies; moreover, about half of these clients have at least one membership in a real estate organization and 5 of them work at a public company.

Regardless of company type, asset class, membership in an organization, or country within the region, the clients who manage and/or invest in commercial real estate properties express an unhindered preference for working with an appraiser on a long-term basis, even though the appraisers mandated by their companies may "differ based on the location, they do not differ by property," as one client notes.

The research conducted reveals that the interests of clients to maintain the partnership with appraisers on a long-term basis can be explained by eight main arguments: communication and trust, the need for flexibility in valuations, company brand of the appraiser, property or asset class, external requirements, avoidance of valuation deviations, information disclosure, and resource-sparing.

Building long-term, trustworthy communication with the appraisers is one of the leading arguments that clients use, and they bring forth the following explanations:

- "We have a history of working together and there is a degree of communication."
- "It is easier . . . we know how the offer looks like and what to expect; we also have a philosophy: if it works, we work with the same partner if he is trustworthy and does his job."
- "You establish a personal level of communication with him."
- "Only efficient . . . when we are a good team."
- "The appraiser knows me and how quickly I want to work."

This intent to have continuous communication is directly related to the need for a certain flexibility or adjustability in the valuation reports. One client working for a small company in Austria in the field of logistics real estate indicates that this is an advantage for "showing him the direction he should follow." Further arguments associated to the need for such flexibilities are the following:

- "I can trust him [the appraiser], he has experience, he knows how far we can discuss with each other about that specific value."
- "Good to work with the same one, to show him the direction."
- "When I make a property acquisition, I trust the appraiser if I know him and he gives me the support I need; for example, if he needs to raise the value with half a point I can influence or convince him easier if I know him already and if I had previously worked with him."
- "We want to have a proper discussion with them [the appraisers], not necessarily to influence them but you have to know what you are talking about and what you can change."
- "Generally speaking I find it better to work with only one appraiser; this has always been good for me because he understands what I want."
- "More open to a discussion."
- "When there is an opportunistic deal, it is important to be able to have the power to influence."
- "Working good together means for me to have the security that the appraiser goes a lot into detail, that he tackles the main points; but he should also have the availability to explain and correct if something is not understandable from my side."
- "Related to transactions now, I want to have a degree of flexibility; I search for a specific value because I need it."
- "Very important that he has the willingness to adapt to your requests and needs."

A further justification given by clients is the importance of the company brand of the appraiser.

- "We work with a big company which does valuations, which has a good image and we trust that they do very good work."
- "We have basically two companies doing valuations, we will add the third one next year; we practically work with the biggest three appraisers."

The next argument lies in the particularity of the property or of the asset class. The clients explain they feel more comfortable when they work with the same appraiser because they get acquainted to the complexity of the asset they need to prepare the valuation report for:

- "It takes time to become experts; it is not easy to change them [the appraisers] because they need time to get to know the special logistics and industrial assets we have in our portfolio."
- "The reason is that he knows what he is doing, he has all the knowledge about the specific asset; we have a long-term partnership with the appraiser and we can trust each other if you know what I mean."

Know-how on the specific property is furthermore seen as another advantage, since this matter also spares time and resources. The clients mention the following motives in this regard:

- "I prefer working with the same appraiser because it spares time sharing information and documents."
- "Working with the same appraiser helps spare resources."
- "He is familiar with the property since he already knows it; and it is not time consuming."
- "If you change him it means that you would have to send more information and the work load is higher."
- "I like to work with the same appraiser because he knows my approach and he knows my properties or projects."

The next argumentation is related to the risk of information disclosure. The clients explain that the exposure rises when appraisers are changed:

- "It is not good for us to change the appraiser because of the risk of information disclosure; even though there is a confidentiality agreement, everyone knows the world is small and such information can be easily transferred."
- "The more the appraiser knows about your properties, the riskier it is to have such information disclosed to third parties; this is why our interest is to keep the same appraiser over a longer period of time."

Additionally, not only is the exposure related to property information higher, the risk of having deviations can rise if the appraiser is changed. The clients disclose the following justifications:

- "I do not change the appraiser often because each of them works with different assumptions."
- "When it comes to the yield and rental income, the appraisers have a different thinking and here come the deviations from."

- "I experienced in the past differences of up to 20% in the valuation of the same real estate asset, and this should not happen."
- "Much easier to work with the same one because he already knows the building, he can estimate much better the whole valuation process; moreover, he also knows much better what my expectations and desires are and in which direction I want to go with the value."
- "When a new appraiser comes there is more effort for us because he questions everything; I have to explain a lot and it takes time until we get used to each other and until he knows the direction I want."

Finally, when the decision to change an appraiser rests solely on the client's decision and not on any external requirement (e.g., from the financing bank), the aim is to work with the same one on a long-term basis as well. The representative of a small client in Austria from the field of logistics real estate concludes in this sense that "our company does not need financing, because we work with our own equity, I have a free choice to assign any appraiser I want; we also do not have to rotate them." The study shows that investors in logistics real estate mostly prefer partnerships with the same appraisers on a long-term basis.

Contrary to the described interests of having a continuous business relationship with the same appraiser throughout a certain period of time, the clients enumerate the occasions when new or different appraisers need to be mandated. Furthermore, 4 clients from small, medium-sized, and large companies explicitly point out that they change the appraiser periodically, in order to precisely avoid valuation extrapolations.

Reasons for changing appraisers can be the following, according to the clients' statements during the interviews:

- *Requirements of the financing banks*: "it always depends on the bank," "we work with the same appraiser, if we do not need a valuation for the bank," "there are some times when you have to work with another one [appraiser] because the financing bank requires it," "if the bank does not consider the valuation report as adequate," and "a bank requires a different or an independent appraiser; the bank uses a certain yield, it has certain demands, this is why we are not bound to one appraiser and work with multiple ones . . . if the third stage – the bank – does not agree to the valuation, I have to change the appraiser; so the bank is the most important player for me."
- *New country or region*: "in the other countries I work with different ones, but they always have to be well-known on the market" and "we work with different appraisers for different assets and locations."
- *Budget*: "at the other company I worked at, which was not listed, we had to make tenders for the appraisers and they were always different; the focus was on the profit center and on the money, we paid for the valuation reports, because the ownership structure was different compared to working for a listed real estate company."

- *New property acquisition*: "if we build up another property fund," "when doing a valuation before the acquisition of an asset I work with different appraisers" and "for a new fund we tender the appraisers and change them."
- *Company's board and/or legal requirements*: "sometimes you have to change the appraisers because the company's Board decided that," "I am working for a big real estate company and the appraisers are chosen by our Board and changed each couple of years," "we are a big international company which is also listed, we have to change the appraisers now and then, so every couple of years; it is a must to do that; but when a appraiser has been assigned for a specific asset or country, we stick with him throughout the whole period and do not change," and "I do what my Board requires – they are in charge with tendering the appraisers, assigning them and negotiating with them."
- *Explicitly not wanting to influence the valuation outcome, therefore seeking for impartial opinions*: "change your appraiser now and then, in order to avoid an extrapolation of the values," "I think it is good to have a 'new look', it keeps you sharp and fresh what values and market information regard," "we do not try to influence the appraiser in any way, we are even well-known for that on the market, because on the long run this can pop up and things can get worse," and "I prefer now to have several opinions and do not follow anybody's interest, so I do not want to stick to an appraiser especially now, when I work for a smaller company; so you change your appraiser when you do not want to have this extrapolation of the same values over and over."

Finally, a clear explanation comes from a client working at a large public real estate company based in Austria, who emphasizes the relevance of working with several appraisers and changing them after a couple of years:

> I find it is an advantage to change them every 2–3 years; otherwise the chances to make a big update are lower because the longer you work with the same one, the more difficult it is to admit that mistakes were made. So, it is good to have a 'refresh' in order to avoid going deeper into something that cannot be repaired after a longer period of time. I can give you an example: after 10 years of working with the same appraiser, the business relationship cannot be very professional. The appraiser always sticks to a certain trend and the valuation report is not real any more. He had his own perception, or he cannot see the mistakes he made, therefore there is a high risk to have a valuation mistake when the appraiser works for you on a long-term. At my current company, since it is a listed company, we have to change the appraisers every couple of years and I think this is good.

4.4.4.3. Client's feedback in commercial property valuation

As shown in the Behavioral Real Estate literature, "client's size affects the willingness to revise, but the magnitude of the client-requested valuation adjustment does not" (Salzman & Zwinkels 2017: 91). The interview outcomes in the field of Behavioral Real Estate are therefore related to the importance appraisers attach to the client's feedback on the property valuation reports they prepare.

"Feedback is essential," according to an appraiser from Romania who works for a large, international agency. Other appraisers working at small, medium-sized, and large companies confirm that and offer extensive explanations that can be summed up into the following justifications:

- *Appraisers are ready to show flexibility and 'adapt' the valuation report*: "I am ready to discuss with the client and if the argument is for me correct, then I am willing to be more flexible" and "I try to establish a good contact with the recurring clients, to adapt to their needs, in order to make them happy and trust me for future valuations; this is why I really try to adapt to their needs."
- *Appraisers indicate the willingness to explain the valuation report and understand their clients' needs*: "when I come to a big difference (10–20%) between my value and the past one I received from the client, I ask the client why; I ask him whether there were other assumptions in the valuation report; it is important to discuss the draft report with your client in order to understand the situation," "feedback of my client is always important and constructive; I always try to reach a consensus with my clients, to explain what I am doing; it is important for me to know that my client is satisfied," and "the feedback is very important for me; I want to be in touch with the client throughout the valuation process and to have a call after I deliver him the final draft."
- *Appraisers' wish is to fulfill the expectations of their clients*: "the key is the relationship you have with the client, the wish of the client to fulfill his targets and the inexistency of the wish to know the value," "we try to win each client, we do what he expects us to do and we try to be fast and deliver quality," "we have a different attitude, we adapt to everything; our behavior towards our clients is generated by the wish to fulfill his wishes," "communication with the client is important, I work with him together and I want him to be satisfied," and "there might be that a client has financing on that certain property but he tells me I should make the valuation without taking this into account; so I do like that but I make sure to write in the assumptions part that the property is valuated without considering the financing."

However, the appraisers show constraint concerning the flexibility or adaptations their clients want them to have in the conducted valuation reports. These constraints are reflected by the awareness of the liability appraisers have towards third parties (e.g., fiscal authorities, banks or judges if the valuation is ordered through court procedures), personal motivations, as well as pressure given by high or unrealistic expectations from clients' side.

Figure 4.12 NVivo Word Cloud – Client's feedback is important for appraisers

Three appraisers who work at small companies illustrate that they are aware of their liability towards third parties when preparing the valuation reports, hence they undertake to be cautious and not risk their professional statute:

- "The question is how much head wind you receive from the other side, especially from the fiscal authorities or from the bank."
- "I have to take care because such valuations go to the judge, if they have been ordered through court . . . for me it is very important that I have a good image and that the judge wants to order the next valuations . . . if you have big deviations you always have a problem, the judge puts this into question and your image might be destroyed."
- "We check the valuations we do for the banks, we discuss with the bank's clients and it is always like that – everyone wants to show a higher equity through a higher value of the property."

Furthermore, appraisers working at small companies explain their own motivations and interests do not to let themselves be influenced by clients:

- "I never forget my liability and my independence."
- "I have an ego problem; I cannot do everything my client wants."
- "I would rather lose a mandate than lose my image or my credibility on the market."
- "I do not want to be too cheap, in order not to distress the market; and I always want to keep my independence and not be influenced by different interests."
- "I avoid a request of a client, if I find it exaggerated, because I want to protect my image and receive further orders."

Figure 4.13 NVivo Word Cloud – Appraiser's flexibility limits

The high pressure or clients' unrealistic expectations is the final argument given by appraisers working at small, medium-sized, and large companies throughout the interviews:

- "Sometimes we do not accept a mandate because the client does not have all necessary documents and they have different expectations which we cannot fulfill from the amounts point of view; 90% of the clients understand, the rest go away."
- "We do not accept pressure, we accept suggestions."
- "There may be also cases when I turn down a mandate because I do not find adequate what the client is requesting from me."
- "We did not take the mandate because we found his expectations to be too high and not appropriate."
- "If a client has an expectation of receiving a value with +30% deviation upwards, I decline."
- "A client wanted full financing from a bank; he wanted a valuation around 30% over the market value, so that he could receive more money from the bank; the clients try to convince you to do that, but I do not accept."
- "I have to feel and understand the client and his needs, if I see he has hidden intentions (for example he insists on a certain price because he needs the valuation for the bank financing), I give up and do not work with him."

4.4.4.4. Relationships between market actors: summary

In this sub-section, the aim is to explain the relationships between the two categories of real estate market actors in commercial property valuation for transaction purposes – the clients (as investors, developers) and the service providers or advisors (as real estate brokers and appraisers).

The first section revealed the outcome of the interviews from an advisors' perspective, who make a distinction between the clients they work for, highlighting the importance of a long-term partnership, as well as the importance they give to the company size or notoriety of the client. Also, the clients emphasize their aim to work with appraisers on a long-term basis.

Finally, these findings are also consistent with previous research on *client's feedback* (Gallimore 1994, 1996; Kinnard 1997; Wolverton & Gallimore 1999; Greiner 2008), about the significance appraisers give to the opinions of their clients on the property valuation reports prepared.

The outcome of this study shows that most of the advisors interviewed make a difference between the partnerships with their clients depending on company size, whereas the difference in their behavior is even deeper when it comes to long-term business relationships versus single mandates. A notable piece of evidence is the fact that most of the service providers who make such a differentiation are the appraisers.

The real estate brokers mention they do a *client screening* before accepting a mandate from a client they haven't worked with before, or from a potential client coming from a small-sized company. Institutional brokers prefer to work with big corporations, whereas the financial situation and trust seem to be the most important arguments for that. The appraisers favor the clients coming from large, well-established companies due to the following argumentations: information availability, professionalism and data quality, financial stability, continuity or ongoing cooperation, transparency, and trust. Furthermore, the service orientation of appraisers towards long-term clients allows a certain *degree of flexibility* for the valuation reports prepared.

Advisors explain that they are cautious with clients they haven't worked with before and thus prefer to maintain long-term business relationships; however, the result of the research also shows that there are other factors besides company size and long-term business relationships for differentiating between clients, from an advisors' perspective, and they are given by the cultural background, the real estate expertise of the client, and the valuation purpose.

Furthermore, part of the original motivation for this research was to shed light on the relationship between appraisers and their clients. Regardless of the company size, the clients who develop and invest in commercial real estate assets express a clear preference for working with appraisers on a long-term basis. This can be explained by eight major arguments: communication and trust, need for flexibility margins in valuation, company's brand of the appraiser, asset class, third-party requirements, avoidance of valuation deviations, information disclosure, and sparing of resources.

On the other hand, the research also reveals the importance appraisers attach to the client's feedback on the property valuation reports they prepare. *Feedback is essential*, and appraisers are ready to show flexibility in adapting the valuation reports and express a willingness to fulfill clients' expectations.

However, the appraisers show that there are certain constraints in their flexibility because of the liability towards third parties such as fiscal authorities, financial institutions, etc., as well as personal motivations (e.g., independence, credibility), or unrealistic expectations from clients.

4.4.5. The generic value drivers of the real estate market actors

The following part of the research conducted aims to explain the value drivers of the real estate market actors (investors, real estate brokers, and appraisers), as an attempt to explain their behavior in the investment decisions undertaken and business relationships.

Numerous biases can be found in corporate real estate valuation processes and generally in the investment decisions.

4.4.5.1. *Investors' value drivers*

The clients enumerate similar interests related to commercial property valuation and appraisal for transaction purposes. The research conducted with 28 clients reveals that the targets and concerns are analogous: special attention is paid to the *yield*, to the *book value* and the directly associated *property valuation report*, but also to *market, portfolio, and asset*-related characteristics, as well as to the *ethics and fairness of the business partners*.

As one client from a large public company explains, a transaction is regarded as a dynamic process, whereas the yield (e.g., profit, return of the investment, cap rate) plays the decisive role. The clients provide notable statements in this regard:

- "Yield is very important . . . its target is usually given by our company."
- "I focus more on the cap rate, because it is the number that remains stable."
- "When I buy an asset, I want a higher yield, otherwise it does not make sense to do the deal."
- "When I buy a property, the yield is definitely an issue because it sets the price . . . it is important for us to see what we can do in order to create the highest return and be over the yield after having improved the property."
- "We do financial engineering and we put equity inside to get certain returns."
- "The profit of the transaction is the most important thing."
- "We work with the principle: there is a deal when there is a profit."
- "Interesting to buy cheap and add value by future investments; or to buy cheap and build additional square meters, so that the value increases, not by a valuation game but by additional investments into the assets."

The *book value (or fair value)* of the transacted property as well as the outcome of the property valuation report are directly associated to the transaction's success, as clients, in particular, reveal:

- "The profit is negative if you sell below the book value; when I sell, I cannot sell below the book value."
- "The best case is when the value remains stable throughout the whole sale process and it should not get higher, otherwise the disposal is not a success anymore; when the fair value is higher, the sale success lowers; it does not

matter, fair value or book value, after the disposal the fair value is introduced directly in the balance sheet."

- "When buying a property, I try to find a way to raise the valuation to an amount higher than the acquisition price; if the price is lower than the fair value at the acquisition point, I have no interest in buying the property; on the other hand, the fair value should not be too low because of the financing (the computation of the loan to value)."
- "The price itself . . . has to be lower than the fair value."
- "Want to pay less than it is worth it."
- "When buying the property, we look to have a high return; this means we want to sell above the book value."
- "When we buy, we think whether the value of that specific value can be increased."
- "When I sell a property, I have to sell it over the fair value; it is a must: either the sale price is higher than the fair value, or the transaction is on hold; in this case I am indeed in contact with my appraiser, I discuss with him the cap rates and the possibilities to adjust them in order to reach a next fair value which is lower, to be able to sell that property."
- "On paper is only a game of the valuation process, for example for showing this to the bank, but it is not real; the potential possible buyers are most of the times not shown in the real value; I call it a valuation game, it can turn out to be positive or negative; it is important not to play this game, in order not to overprice a property; if it is overpriced, the crisis will come soon."
- "Target that the value has to remain constant or even to go up; when you change the appraiser, given the same market environment, and you assign another one from the big ones, you come to different values in transactions; a valuation report is necessary for an investor in order to base himself on a specific number, so he wants a number, not an opinion or a clarification";
- "The rule is: the valuation must not be below the acquisition price and we have to look at the development of the asset in the next 8–10 years; when we sell, the price has to be higher than the valuation amount."
- "We want to have correct numbers but of course we are interested in an upward valuation, and the inflation and interest rates always need to be considered, they play a psychological role."
- "Values are very important, and they are mainly given by the rental income. The property values must remain stable and have a slight increase over the years, in order to reach a higher profit when you sell the assets. Otherwise it is very hard to receive the prices you want if they are overvalued."
- "If the fair value is too high and the property cannot be sold, one has to find a way to force it down if the property is on the disposal list."
- "The challenge has been to adapt the values to the market, in many cases the valuations did not correspond to the real estate market; but after many negotiations with the appraisers, after several findings and pressure made by the Board, they eventually replied to our needs."

The second significant interest of the real estate market actors who manage and invest in commercial property in Austria and Central and Eastern Europe lies in the attention paid to the information regarding *market, portfolio, and asset strategy*. The availability of data is critical and, as a client from a large company investing in logistics real estate in the CEE region illustrates, having up-to-date market information is of utmost importance:

> Even when we are not directly involved in a certain deal, or we do not want to buy the asset, we often participate in order to gain some information and know the price; anyway, we are aware that the information can never be perfect or complete.

Two clients explain further that "after SPA signing, the highest risk is to have loses if certain needed information was not disclosed on time, so our interest is to avoid such circumstances and share all needed information, mostly in the form of due diligence," so "data plays a role, but when there is something which we need and is not there, we agree on retentions or deductions."

Further on, clients focus on the *asset-related characteristics* during a transaction, and these can be classified into:

- *Technical features*: Building specifications, design, footprint, additional land to construct on, refurbishment opportunities, location, and functional characteristics (e.g., delivery gates in the case of logistics real estate entrance, signage, catchment area in the case of retail properties).
- *Portfolio and asset strategy*: Performance of the asset or of the investment fund, the product to match the strategy, long-term performance, and the management capacity of the seller to operate the building.
- *Sustainability*: Green certificates.
- *Income*: Sustainable rental income, leasing situation and tenant-mix, marketing budget for retail properties, service charges composition, and property valuation as a "constant, sustainable increase."

The third important evidence concerning client objectives in a transaction is a reference to *business ethics*, justified by the clients' expectations from their business partners to be reliable and have professional business conduct. The expertise of the consultants and lawyers, together with the liquidity of the buyer and his financing power, are also fundamental milestones for the clients interviewed. The need for transparency is very often expressed by clients, with one client pointing out that the transparency and the rules of business conduct in the real estate field are decisive for fair execution which leads to the transaction completion.

Furthermore, the clients have explicit expectations from appraisers to "be flexible and be able to adapt," to "support the targets thorough the valuation process, before and after the transaction," and from the real estate brokers to "make pressure on the counter-party and fasten the transaction process."

The necessity to have a fast transaction process is underpinned by the remarks coming from several clients: "when I have a property and really have to sell it, I do not pay attention to many factors, I want to sell it fast," "if I want to maximize my profit from the sale, I want to have a fast transaction process," "even though it is more energy consuming, it has to be fast, otherwise you cannot accomplish your targets," and it is important that the "transaction is done fast and at the agreed terms."

Finally, clients offer evidence and express several concerns regarding the business environment:

- "The rent free period does not appear in the contract, but in a side letter, this is why the appraiser cannot reflect the reality; the market situation is distressed, because the net effective rent should be evaluated and it isn't; we are concerned with that . . . it is hard for us to compete in such non-transparent markets, it is indeed a challenge."
- "It might happen that the construction works are stopped, and the company requires an additional 5% payment in order to restart the construction; in Austria it is easier, you have a more efficient and faster enforceability but in Eastern Europe is takes much longer and is more complicated."

Besides the evidence on the problems related to the real estate business environment, one client explains that transparency can be of concern due to the dual function of the real estate broker, who represents both contractual parties and might have biased interests. A client concluded by explaining, "I do not know which party he represents and what interests he has."

4.4.5.2. Brokers' value drivers

A long-term business relationship with the clients is highlighted by the real estate brokers, who explain that the continuous contact with loyal and serious partners on a trustworthy basis is an essential milestone for the business continuity:

- "I want to have the best contact with my clients, otherwise I am the one who suffers; I try to have a long-term business relationship with him, win-win is maybe too much, it has to be at least a 'no dead body policy.'"
- "I prefer to deal with both parties in a transaction, because I know how to read people, so this personal approach is important for me to have a synchronization – price, standard, time."
- "I want to continue the relationship, it is important to keep a good cooperation, even though you are not always paid; for example, once we helped although we knew the client did not pay us; he was happy with that deal and we received from him a fee at the next deal."
- "I prefer the transactions with recurrent business, where you can establish a relationship and develop it for further deals."

- "The long-term relationship, the repetitive business with the client is important but the synchronicity is also important; the client selection is very expensive . . . it costs me more to attract a new client than to work with the old one."

Brokers explain throughout the interviews that information availability (data quality) and confidentiality are essential in their business. One notable remark comes from an international real estate broker who admits "you command the stock, you command the market; so information availability is very important."

Ethics is directly linked to the accuracy of data; in this sense, the brokers highlight the importance of loyalty and confidentiality ("through the internationalization a lot of things are uncovered").

Further value drivers for real estate brokers lie in:

- *The identified property features*: marketable, "the property has to be liquid, to be sellable quickly," location, property title, "potential deals with the tenants of the property are important and interesting," and "condition of the building, zoning and permitted use, extensions possible or restrictions."
- *Brokerage fee*: "establish the fee right from the beginning," "my interest is that the prices are higher, but we have to be realistic," "my scope is to obtain a good deal and I want to know right from the beginning who is paying the fee," and "get the deal done."
- *Timeframe*: "the time is important, the duration until the deal comes to a closing" and "speed of the deal."
- *Personal success*: prestige, "I also want to make a good, professional impression for further recommendations and further business," and "my clients want to work with reputable brokers and I have to show that and act accordingly."

On the other hand, the concerns of the real estate brokers also have implications in their behavior, and these are directly related to market practice and to the other market actors.

Finally, some real estate brokers assess the generic market environment and express their concerns when making the difference between small and large agencies, or between market actors in general:

- "In commercial real estate, only a small part of the market participants works on a trustworthy basis."
- "Big brokers send artificial inquires to local, small brokers even though there is no basis; they ask for certain properties with certain specifications; then a feedback comes from these smaller brokers; with this information they go to the tenants (especially the big occupiers in logistics); if a positive signal comes from a tenant, the big brokers would eventually contact investors, telling them that the logistics company X has interest for the location Y."
- "An example of conflict of interest: I have an office building to let and the tenant wants me to represent him; on the other side, since we are a big

company, we have another department dealing with the investor's representation; the first thing I have to do is to disclose to my team that I have a mandate to market the building and to inform both the owner and the tenant that two divisions within our company deal with the project; so I want to establish a contractual clause with the tenant I represent, to make sure I am covered about the fact that my other department is representing the counterparty, the owner; on the other hand, we give a notice also to the owner that I represent the tenant; so you have to navigate in this relationship between owner and tenant; this is especially important when dealing with international companies."

- "The big agencies do another thing – when it does not work with a transaction they leave this to the smaller brokers, because they know the smaller brokers want to be more honest and they work more for their fee."

Furthermore, the brokers complain that the banks "do not pay a high fee" and they compare themselves to other service providers such as lawyers, who "are paid by hour" while they are "only paid if the deal takes place." One real estate broker points out, "sometimes the lawyers make problems and forget that the target is to get the contract signed."

The real estate brokers are also concerned with the behavior of their clients and adapt themselves to that:

- "Big corporations have a lot of procedures and are very formal; they only disclose information when they have a need, because they want to protect the transaction or the business."
- "I hate when different investors come to me just to double-check the market, if I see the request is not real, I draw back."
- "When I see that the partnership or the property is difficult, I know the work is in vain, so I draw back."
- "Communication problems with investors, they also do not disclose many things . . . their interest is to see what clients they might have and whether a deal might be concrete."
- "Cannot trust the client."
- "There are lots of companies who contact brokers just to find out details about the market or about a certain property."
- "Big real estate companies often do a market research, they only make inquiries in order to find out what properties are on the market and at which price."
- "There are many investors that do not have correct information, or others that do not want to give this information to brokers; for example, they do not want to give the floor plans and they keep this confidential; so this is why I do not give everything to my other clients, because information is missing or is incomplete and I want to work in a professional manner."

- "The worst thing is to have two appraisers working for the same property at the same time; when both sides (buyer, seller) instruct me to do the valuation I am more objective and transparent because the data quality is better; when this comes only from one party, I have to trust the documents received."

A last statement on third parties' opinions and involvement related to valuation reports comes from an appraiser working at a large brokerage and advisory company: "another advantage is when the buyer and the seller can use the same valuation report, one to show it to the bank and the other one to the Supervisory Board."

4.4.5.4. *Summary*

As a final note, the target of this chapter was to identify and explain the value drivers of the real estate market actors. This has been split by investor, real estate broker, and appraiser, explaining the objectives they want to reach as well as the concerns related to the business environment and market practices.

The investors interviewed have similar views when it comes to property valuation and appraisal for transaction purposes; here, special attention is paid to the yield, book value, and result of the valuation report, property or asset class, market environment, and ethics and fairness of the business partners.

By contrast, their main concerns are expressed by the rather non-transparent real estate markets in Central and Eastern Europe (given by the commercial and legal aspects such as rent-free periods, enforceability of bad debts, etc.). Finally, the dual function of the real estate broker is questioned, due to the biases that arise when a broker represents two parties (buyer and seller of real estate property).

From a broker's perspective, a long-term relationship and continuous contact with the client are essential milestones for the success of the business. Furthermore, besides data quality and information availability ("you command the stock, you command the market"), the value drivers for brokers are given by the following aspects: brokerage fee, property easy to be marketed, timeframe, and personal success. The concerns explained by the real estate brokers lie on one hand, in the market practice and the business ethics; on the other hand, they are related to the legal framework or to the fact that the financial institutions generally commit to lower fees for the brokerage services.

Finally, the appraisers, like the real estate brokers, highlight the significance of their long-term business relationship with their clients. The appraisers want to maintain a trustworthy relationship with their clients, need data transparency for the valuation reports they prepare, and highlight the fact that the fee and the work load need to be settled at the beginning of the mandate.

Moreover, the opinions of third parties and the fact that the valuation outcome needs to be validated by external authorities (e.g., fiscal institutions) play a significant role for the appraisers. Their complaint lies mostly in the client's pressure, either because of the time frame or because of the valuation expectations expressed by the clients.

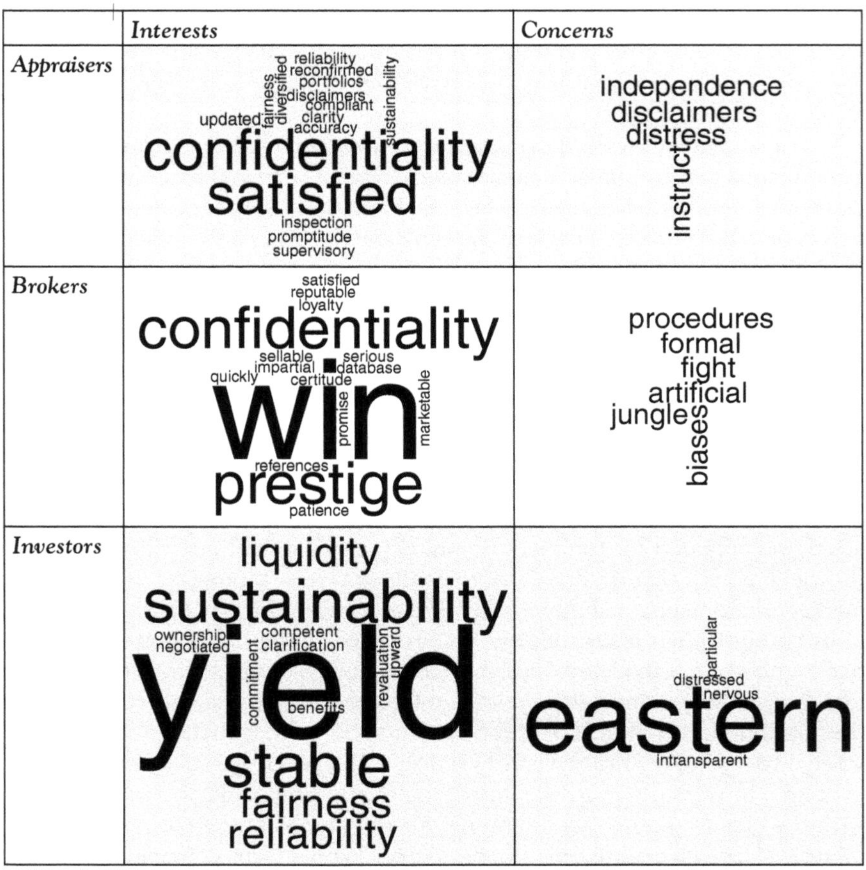

Figure 4.14 NVivo Word Cloud – Interests and concerns of the market actors

The figure above illustrates the value drivers as well as the concerns of the real estate market actors as an outcome of the qualitative analysis conducted with NVivo.

Bibliography

Gallimore, Paul (1994): Aspects of Information Processing in Valuation Judgement and Choice. *Journal of Property Research*. Vol. 11. No. 2

Gallimore, Paul (1996): Confirmation Bias in the Valuation Process: A Test for Corroborating Evidence. *Journal of Property Research*. Vol. 13. No. 4

Graaskamp, James A. (1977): *The Appraisal of 25 N. Pinckney: A Demonstration Case for Contemporary Appraisal Methods*. Madison, WI: Landmark Research

Greiner, Martin (2008): Kapitel 4.1.3. Verhaltenstheorie: Behavioral Real Estate, in Schulte, Karl-Werner (ed.) *Immobilienökonomie*. Band IV. Volkswirtschaftliche Grundlagen. München: Oldenbourg

Kinnard, William N. et al. (1997): Client Pressure in the Commercial Appraisal Industry: How Prevalent Is It? *Journal of Property Valuation and Investment*. Vol. 15. No. 3

Salzman, Diego & Zwinkels, Remco (2017): Behavioral Real Estate. *Journal of Real Estate Literature*. Vol. 25. No. 1

Wolverton, Marvin L. & Gallimore, Paul (1999): Client Feedback and the Role of the Appraiser. *Journal of Real Estate Research*. Vol. 18. No. 3

5 Findings for Principal-Agent theory and moral hazard in real estate

5.1. Introduction

In addition to the behavioral theories and evidence in commercial property valuation, the present study also focuses on the information asymmetries between the real estate market actors. It aims to reveal whether there exist such information asymmetries between the market actors (either between investors or developers and real estate brokers, or between investors or developers and appraisers) before and after having signed a contract for a property transaction or for a valuation (e.g., Sale-Purchase Agreement, Letter of Intent, binding and non-binding agreements, mandates for commercial property valuation, Brokerage Agreement).

This chapter is organized as follows. In the first section, the behavior of the real estate market actors is presented, focusing on the information they disclose before signing a contract (between investors or developers as Principal, and real estate broker or appraiser as Agent). This will be presented from the investors' (as buyers and sellers of commercial property assets), brokers' (as advisors in real estate transactions), as well as appraisers' (as service providers of property valuation reports) point of view.

The present study confirms that there are information asymmetries between the market actors and tries to develop a set of rules indicating what type of information is not disclosed before and after having signed a contract between Principal and Agent.

The second section of the chapter presents the outcome of the interviews with 52 real estate market actors and the information shared between each other after having signed a contract or a mandate. The results demonstrate that while the Principals (investors, developers) and the real estate brokers (the first category of Agents) still retain information after concluding an agreement, the appraisers (the second category of Agents) try to show which type of information is withheld from the Principals' side, while maintaining a high level of transparency towards their clients.

5.2. Before a binding or a non-binding agreement

5.2.1. *Investors*

The investors illustrate general statements related to the transaction process and the information known or disclosed before signing a binding agreement. One of them discloses that "we always take into consideration the potential buyer when we disclose such data." Other investors outline the information asymmetries in transactions, such as:

- "When I sell a property, it helps a lot if the last positive market development of the asset is not present in the last valuation report; in this way a disposal over the fair value takes place; for example, the fair value is 5.5 M. Euro but the market is 'ready' to pay 5.75 for it; it can get problematic when the disposal process with the conducted Due Diligence takes several months."
- "The rent income might be true, but also what you spend is important; so in most cases you might have a surprise at the beginning."
- "An example: the value of land is 'x' but there come additional 30 Euro per sqm as development fee for the state (in Slovenia for example); so you do not get the full picture and it is up to you to find out the full price."

Furthermore, there are investors who disclose that they might participate in certain transaction processes just for the sake of finding out market information, without necessarily wanting to buy the specific property:

- "Even when we are not directly involved in a certain deal, or we do not want to buy the asset, we often participate in order to gain some information and know the price; anyway, we are aware that the information can never be perfect or complete."
- "Big real estate companies often do some kind of a market study, they only make inquiries in order to know what properties are on the market and at which price."

The next part of this chapter will present the opinions of the buyers and sellers of real estate properties concerning the information they share with service providers such as appraisers and real estate brokers.

When working together with appraisers in real estate transactions or for property valuations, the investors disclose the types of information that are not directly shared between their companies and the mandated appraisers. According to the opinion of two investors, "it would be too ambitious to say that we give our appraisers 100% information" and "I give them only information which I consider relevant for the valuation."

To continue, the investors avoid communicating the following (full) property-related information during the valuation process:

- Rental income.
- Void period.
- Rent free periods or the rent reduction agreements made for a short or medium term.
- Capital expenditure.
- "Soft sides" such as how good (related to credit worthiness, image etc.) the tenants are, or how high the expectations.

- The appraiser should not necessarily know that an acquisition is planned.
- The investors claim that in CEE the appraisers can be more flexible, especially in adjusting the yields and rental income assumptions.

However, there are investors who claim they are transparent with the appraisers, but not with the real estate brokers. Before illustrating the information shared with the brokers – from an investor's perspective – it is relevant to note that the investors interviewed express the need to be fully transparent to the appraisers because of the mandatory audits and the strict regulations of real estate investment funds: "transparent relationship with my appraisers, we are regulated as real estate fund and we have a duty to disclose everything" and "we have constant audits so we really have to be very transparent and to give the appraiser each information he needs." The investors claim that the transparency also rises after having signed a confidentiality agreement (or non-disclosure agreement) with the appraiser beforehand.

Furthermore, the buyers and sellers of commercial property disclose a fully different behavior and perception related to the real estate brokers involved in a transaction. There are investors who point out the risk of information asymmetries or of different interests when having a property valuation done by the same company involved in the commercialization of an asset:

- "I mostly work with big companies and normally they have a department for valuation, a department for brokerage of commercial, residential properties etc.; when I ask the appraiser to do a valuation report for a standing investment, I get an independent view and a certain value; but when I ask – within the same company – the brokerage department, I get a higher estimated value because they want to obtain the mandate to sell the property; so I receive two different numbers for the same property; one is so to say the independent one, whereas the value for a property on the disposal list is estimated to be higher so that the broker can get assigned for that disposal; in the end the sale price is normally lower, but the broker won his mandate."
- "In situations when our appraiser is also a broker (this is the case for the big agencies), I want to go to another independent appraiser in order to get precise information; I do not believe in the Chinese wall, I am sure they have their own interests."
- "I want to go to another independent appraiser in order to get precise information. I do not believe in the Chinese wall."
- "I find it very controversial when I deal with big agencies which also have a valuation department, I do not believe in the Chinese wall at all, it simply does not exist; the appraiser knows the rental income and the contractual periods and he always goes to his colleague from the brokerage department and such information is shared with him; the information is not kept confidential and this is why such big agencies have a comparative market advantage, because they know a lot about the market and they can even dictate very well; the broker, as colleague of his appraiser, receives too much

information on the asset and this is what I do not like at all and what I cannot trust."
- "When I had to sell an office property, I compiled a file with all relevant information about the property, and then I gave it to the broker; it was clear that the broker did not have time to invest in writing so many details, but my interest was to sell the property so I wanted to have correct and transparent information; but: in this case the broker was also my appraiser, here is the difference, this is why I shared with him all information on the property."

Most of the evidence related to the information asymmetry between market players in commercial property valuation and transactions comes from the interviews carried out with real estate investors (as clients) and real estate brokers (as service providers).

The investors interviewed show a generic lack of trust towards real estate brokers and very often put into question to what extend a broker is ready to represent their commercial interests:

- "The broker is into the fee he might get, but the deal might not be the best one."
- "The broker tries to close the deal using as little resources as possible and he pushes both seller and buyer; he actually pushes the party with whom he assumes he has more success with."
- "I would not rely on a broker immediately; the due diligence is very important, and it is our responsibility."
- "When I buy a property the assistance of a broker is very low, most of the times the data room where all the documents should be found has a bad quality."
- "The chances that the broker really represents your interests are very low, it does not mean I exclude the broker, but I do not send him any information in a direct manner."

The investors denounce the incomplete information received from brokers ("do not pass all relevant information about an asset or a specific transaction," "it may happen that the information we receive about a property is false," "the classic problems when dealing with the brokers are definitely the lack of information about the tenant situations and their contract prolongations," "they are waiting to receive their fee but they do not have a good performance, they do not really work at the deal," "they do not even know how high the service charges are," and "the brokers do not have an interest to raise the price when they have to sell a property for me, they are only interested in the disposal itself, as soon as they found an interested buyer") and illustrate their reasons for being cautious with the property information shared by disclosing the type of basic information they usually distribute to brokers in commercial property transactions. Valuation reports, information regarding tenants having cancelled a lease agreement, project timeline, and capital expenditure are examples of information not shared with the real estate brokers.

On the contrary, buyers of real estate properties want to disclose little information (even after signing an NDA), and they restrict it to data on location, total area, approximate rental price, or rental income. A couple of interviewees pointed out the importance of indemnity or penalty clauses in the NDAs signed with real estate brokers and add "in Austria you have to have some sanctions if you want to be sure that the information does not go to the market and is made official."

Furthermore, while the markets in CEE as considered to be non-transparent ("there are a lot of interactions with brokers, if we pay the fee we get the info," according to one investor from CEE), the buyers and sellers of real estate properties consider the dual function of brokers in Austria problematic ("problems in the information distribution because the broker works practically for both parties and you cannot exactly know on which side he really is and what interest he really has"); however, based on the opinion of an Austrian investor, there is a current market trend that the broker represents only one party in commercial real estate transactions.

Investors further indicate the preference not to conclude exclusivity agreements with brokers ("you lose the time and there is no competition between the brokers," "if a market is difficult, you should not have exclusivity," and "the broker catches you in such a contract and you cannot know whether he really works for you"); on the other hand, they mention it is important to clarify right from the beginning the party who pays the commission and agree on a certain fee with the broker in order to have better service quality ("in case I assign him with a search I am more transparent, but still not disclose everything," "the sooner he manages to find a buyer and the transaction takes place, the higher the fee and more convenient the payment terms," and "the higher the achieved sale price, the higher the fee they get").

A last remark from the interviews conducted with investors in commercial properties is related to the difference made between small and large renowned agencies. While the small brokers are considered to have a bad image and be superficial, the institutional investors illustrate openness to larger agencies because they "support the deals and act as mediators" or they "know the international tenants very well and find out if a tenant is willing to prolong his contract or not."

As a final note, three interviewees wrap up the problems when working with brokers in commercial real estate transactions by illustrating the problems after having assigned a broker for buying or selling an asset:

- "For the broker counts everything what happens before a contract signing, afterwards he completely loses the interest, as soon as he knows his fee will be paid."
- "Brokers are active until you signed the LOI to make a deal, after they establish the contact between seller and buyer they draw back; this is a problem in my opinion, because they do not give you support any more."

- "The brokers often show in a too positive way, in order to get to the fee, he might even tell you the vacancy rate of a property is not important, by mentioning that his colleagues would find new tenants very easily; this is how a broker wants to convince you to make the deal."

5.2.2. *Appraisers*

Before commencing a contractual agreement for property valuation, the appraisers raised three main topics they want to settle beforehand: negotiation and agreement upon the fee (if no framework agreement is in place), preparation of a draft calculation in order to estimate the expectations of the client as well as to assess the difficulty of the valuation report, in terms of information availability, type of property, or client.

The appraisers want to clarify the clients' intentions and expectations by preparing a draft calculation before signing the contract for delivering the valuation report:

- "A short analysis in which I tell him the approximate value and if he has no interest to continue because the value is not what he expected, I stop and I do not work for him."
- "I make the draft, then I finalize it and I document everything; there is some place for a deviation of some percentages in the final fine tuning."
- "We normally prepare a draft with the value and we want to clarify in advance with the client whether this is according to his expectations; we define in this offer phase the documents we need, the timeframe and the rough estimation on the value."

In addition to the statements concerning the drafts appraisers might prepare before a contractual agreement with a client, there is evidence on the fact that they might also have to decline a mandate when the expectations of the party ordering the valuation report are not in accordance with their opinions as appraisers:

- "It happened several times that I had to decline mandates because the clients wanted to have a higher value than I could deliver."
- "A client wanted to buy a property which had a single tenant inside; in Austria, you have lease agreements for an undefined period of time and in this case, my opinion was that the rent level was not sustainable and couldn't be achieved on a long-term, especially if the current tenant left the building; so I had to make a discount in the valuation; in my opinion the property was over-rented and my potential client wanted me to calculate the value with a higher rental level, as the client wanted to purchase that property; I had to decline the mandate because for me this was not justifiable, and in the end it is me who is liable for the valuations I deliver."

Finally, the appraisers aim to prepare valuation reports which are not demanding or complicated. For that, they pay attention to the property type and information availability ("if it's too complicated or the data is missing, it takes more time for me; the office and industrial properties are similar, but in retail, something new comes up all the time" and "if a building is under construction, the valuation is more complicated; you have to work with the residual value and it takes a lot of time because of the deviations").

Furthermore, a subject matter the appraisers are careful about concerns the clients or partners they work with ("I want uncomplicated clients – if the desire is complicated, it's more work for me" and "I prefer to deal with bigger companies, with larger portfolios because it is much easier – the valuation assumptions are similar, the communication is only with one party, it is easier to handle"), and note that the valuation is even less complicated when there is only one appraiser in charge during the transaction process:

> what is important for me is that I know that I am the only appraiser for a property; in such a case I receive all necessary information, otherwise I might not receive all that I want because the other party has another appraiser and maybe different interests.

5.2.3. *Real estate brokers*

The real estate brokers constitute the last category of real estate market actors interviewed with the aim of investigating the behavior and interests before concluding an agreement with an investor (buyer or seller of real estate assets) or real estate developer. Similar to the appraisers, as previously described, the real estate agents have the interest to first settle the fee before entering into a contractual agreement ("we have a pressure and this is the fee," "it is important how the fee is split," and "it is given by the transaction price and it must be negotiated right from the beginning, in order to avoid conflicts or misunderstandings afterwards").

Along with that, the brokers mention that the LOI is decisive and, as one broker discloses, "I am more relaxed and work less as soon as I got him to sign the LOI; as soon as my client signs the LOI, there is less work for me."

Another similarity to appraisers is the fact that the brokers also want to have easy and fast transactions (or properties):

- "If I believe in a property and I am convinced the transaction will be done soon, I present it to as many clients as possible; if I do not think or estimate that, I do not even start working on it, I just keep it in my files, in order to have the information about it."
- "Then, if the request is too small . . . I cannot help but I keep this kind of request in my portfolio overview and not negate it from the beginning; it may be that something would appear in the future, so it would be a pity to negate a deal."
- "If I deal with a third city and I know it is difficult to market it, I do not start my work. I tell to me client I won't do that, I'm sorry; the property has to be easy to be commercialized, otherwise you lose your time; the property needs

to be interesting enough in order to be sold; it also has to do with the price expectation – clients have sometimes very high expectations and nothing happens, afterwards they say it is the fault of the broker because he was not able to sell the property."

The previous statement, given by an experienced broker, is in direct connection the next topic – the expected sale price. Here, the brokers might want to convince the buyer to lower the transaction price in order to facilitate a transaction:

- "I try to convince the investor that the market value should be lower, in order to get the deal done."
- "When a lot of time goes by and the property was not sold, I also try to convince the client to lower the book value."
- "Before making the pitch to convince them they sign the contract with you, you have to explain very well why the price is like that."

A last decisive argument for brokers before entering an agreement with their clients is given by the information availability and how they manage it. On one hand, there are brokers who mention that they have to disclose the name of their client upfront in order to "show reliability towards other business partners" or be competitive.

On the other hand, brokers also complain about the false or insufficient property information they receive from their clients: "the description of the property does not match its actual condition, especially the technical status is worse than previously indicated, the indexation is not correct or there are problems with the tenancies and the prolongation of the lease agreements."

The real estate brokers interviewed were further asked if there was property data they would not disclose in order to not hinder a transaction. Along with the tenancy situation and information regarding the balance sheet or composition of the turnover, the real estate brokers interviewed emphasize the following situations:

- "If you hear that a building near the property you market will be destroyed, you should disclose that only if you can prove the information is correct; if you cannot give the proof, you should not tell this to your client."
- "Many brokers make the so called yield compression, they tell to their potential client the price in 6 months, not the actual price; it is a mistake to mention the present price, so you can push your luck and say later 'I'm sorry that the market did not go in that direction, it's the fault of the market.'"
- "The broker's strategy depends on the situation, if you are on a buyer market, you make the property more expensive and so get a higher fee, but when there is a seller market, you go lower with the price and the deal is more rapid."
- "I would not disclose when the early access is planned, if I know the background of the investor."

- "If you market a property and you do not know for sure when it will be finished, you do not disclose such thing."
- "It could be a mistake to disclose data like technical specifications or layout; you could have problems with the commercialization afterwards if you disclose that too fast."
- "Rental status – this is information that I keep for me and do not disclose to the investor at the beginning."

5.3. After concluding a binding or a non-binding agreement

5.3.1. *Investors*

The interviews carried out with investors show that the information transparency towards real estate brokers is still not completely fulfilled. Especially the sellers of real estate properties illustrate the type of data that is not disclosed to a broker, even after having signed the SPA or even a binding LOI:

> There might be information that I would still not disclose, for example if there had been some agreements with a certain tenant and it is not necessary for the new owner to have such information; specifically, if former agreements with tenants do not affect the transaction and the property, I do not disclose such information, even after signing the SPA.

"But I still hold back important or strategic information if we have a hint that someone wants to use it (lease income and everything related to the tenants, lease agreement, contract)."

While the investors still tend to retain strategic information that is usually tenant-related, they show full transparency with the appraisers, the second category of real estate service providers:

> we give our appraisers all necessary information, we even tell them the final sales price, for their documentation and reference values; there is a high degree of information exchange with the appraiser as opposed to the broker, on a confidentiality basis.

Despite that, an investor indicates that "my disclaimer is, it should not be pointed out explicitly towards the negative circumstance."

5.3.2. *Appraisers*

After having received the mandate for property valuation, the appraisers still criticize the lack of transparency in the information or property data received from their clients. In the interviews, the appraisers indicate that the clients usually do not disclose material that is relevant for the valuation report:

- "I always receive too much data or too little; when a property is sold, you can have tons of documents in the data room which do not have a proper description; also the seller, he wants you to think that is making everything available but in fact he isn't."
- "there are costs for such refurbishment that might arise and these costs influence the valuation report and outcome; the appraiser needs to know such costs (which are again reflected in the NOI afterwards), but there are many clients who do not disclose that."
- "the clients do not give the previous valuation reports, they would not disclose such reports if they were done by other appraisers or they only disclose the result, the specific value, but don't give the whole report."
- "the problems with a neighbor shouldn't be disclosed or taken into account."
- "in the case of the one-time clients, there are a lot of problems with the data quality; it is hard to receive the complete lease agreements, the plans, you have to make the study on your own, you have to make more assumptions and have more disclaimers, so it is very difficult and time-consuming."

At an international level, in the case of the companies which have an international (at least CEE-based) network, the information necessity is not severe because the appraisers make use of the data received from their colleagues: "we always evaluate properties where we have data evidence, or we do our own study . . . we have a track-record of many properties since we have this international network."

Finally, a last concern of appraisers after signing the mandate and during the delivery period is the time pressure coming from their clients: "I want to decide for myself when I am ready, I do not want that an authority comes and gives me a certain deadline, as long as I am not sure whether I will have all information on time."

5.3.3. *Real estate brokers*

The evidence coming from the interviews conducted with real estate brokers shows three important aspects elucidated after the mandate for a property disposal has been signed.

First, the brokers note that they are "more relaxed and work less" as soon as the Letter of Intent between a buyer and a seller in a property transaction is signed. A broker explained that

> as soon as my client signs the LOI, there is less work for me; the fee is important and this is settled in the LOI as well, so you tend to be more relaxed when the LOI is signed, because at this point the parties normally start to negotiate with each other and you are less involved in such negotiations.

Second, contrary to the skeptical opinions of investors about the broker's dual function, the real estate brokers prefer it because they want to have the lead: "the higher the transaction or the contract volume, the more I want to be in direct contact with both seller and buyer; I prefer to be a dual agent because I can control things better."

Third, the real estate brokers start negotiating on the price with the other parties and are inclined to lower the expectations of the clients concerning property disposals by lowering the target price in the discussions with other real estate market participants:

- "There are owners who come and demand let's say 45 Euro per sqm, although we say this is much above the market; we tell the specific owner that we do not know anyone to pay so much for a land in that specific location; we say to ourselves 'we lose our time but ok, let's give it a try'; and then we sign the brokerage agreement, which is important for us; time goes by, the offers (normally much lower) come, the owner (our client) starts to negotiate after a while, and we finally come to an agreement; it would work like that: the owner says 45 Euro, we sign the brokerage agreement anyway, the best offer is 28 Euro, the owner says 33 and so we can meet in the middle at 30 Euro/sqm; so it takes time but the brokerage agreement is important to be signed."
- "The owners come to us with higher demands, but we manage to sell – normally at a lower price."
- "An investor once had an exaggerated expectation in my view; he wanted to receive a price of 75 M Euro, I found that totally excessive; when such thing happens I am not interested because I know I work in vain; but I went to a potential buyer and told him like that: 'consider this 75 M is a joke, my price and my truth is 62 M'; the parties seem to have accepted that and they are now in the due diligence process."

5.4. Conclusions

Part of the original reason for this study was to supply evidence of the information asymmetries – if any – between the real estate market actors, which were divided into three main categories (real estate investors or property developers as Principals and real estate brokers as well as advisors as Agents) in the field of commercial property valuation and transactions.

Moreover, the aim of this paper was to shed light and explain the interests and motivations of the market actors, using the Principal-Agent theory and moral hazard as domains of study that have been examined to a rather small extent so far.

In the first part of the chapter, the behavior of the market actors before entering into a contractual agreement was presented, with the focus on the information asymmetries that arise because of the fact that certain information might not be disclosed. Specifically, it has been shown that both Principals and Agents are led by their own interests, and that makes them retain certain type of information in commercial property transactions and valuations.

The investors in real estate assets disclose on one hand, the fact that their interest is to have a property disposal over the fair value, and thus their target in this case is that the positive development of the asset is not shown in the last valuation report; and on the other hand, they explain that they might participate at certain transaction processes in order to acquire market information, and not because of a real interest for a property acquisition.

First, in the communication with their appraisers, the Principals avoid disclosing several pieces of information on their assets such as: void periods, rent-free periods made for a short or medium term, total capital expenditure, *soft information* such as future expectations on the tenancy situation, and planned acquisitions. Moreover, the Principals are cautious when they know that the appraiser works together in the same agency involved in the commercialization of the properties.

Finally, the institutional investors, such as real estate funds (e.g., REIT's), explain that there is full transparency with the appraisers in the case of mandatory audits (so not directly related to the transaction purpose), due to the strict regulations of investment funds.

The Principals show an even deeper lack of confidence in their cooperation with the real estate brokers in real estate transactions. They note that the information received from brokers has a bad quality and, therefore, they tend to not trust what they receive up to the point when a due diligence study is conducted. Valuation reports, information regarding tenants having cancelled a lease agreement, the development project timeline, or capital expenditure are examples of information not disclosed to the real estate brokers.

Furthermore, the Principals point out the importance of establishing indemnity or penalty clauses in the brokerage contracts in order to avoid information disclosure; they also try to avoid concluding exclusivity agreements because in such case there is no competition on the market.

The investors also mark the difference between small and large corporations (agencies), and tend to trust the second category, since such agencies very often offer support as mediators between buyers and sellers. A final issue is highlighted by the Principal's concern about the Agent's dual function in Austria and overall concern related to the non-transparent and non-regulated real estate markets of CEE, where the broker's function and fee are not directly and specifically defined by national laws or regulations.

Second, the appraisers raise three main concerns before concluding a contract for a valuation mandate with the Principal: the initial definition of the fee, the necessity to prepare a draft calculation in order to estimate the client's expectations, and the assessment of the difficulty of the valuation process – related to information availability, type of property, and client. In this last regard, the appraisers mention that the "easy" valuation mandates are favored, which are not as time-consuming.

The real estate brokers provide extensive examples of the information that is not disclosed before entering into a contractual agreement (very often Letter of Intent). The brokers are interested in the commercialization of properties which are easy to be sold, and want to avoid working in vain, so they try to convince the buyer or the seller to lower the transaction price (or in many cases the book value) in order to speed up the process.

Moreover, the brokers also complain that the information received from their Principals is very often incorrect or not complete; they disclose the fact that they tend to not reveal the following information on a property in order not to hinder its disposal: tenancy situation, balance sheet, turnover, the market situation of the neighboring buildings, information on the early access regarding properties under development, and detailed technical specifications and layouts.

Finally, the brokers want to make a property more expensive in a buyer's market in order to achieve a higher fee (and in a seller's market, less expensive so that the deal can take place). The *yield compression* is also an element that might be used, especially by large international agencies who possess extended market information and try in this way to assess a potential future acquisition price, so to achieve a higher fee leverage.

The second section of the chapter presents the outcome of the interviews carried out with real estate market actors in order to assess the information asymmetries after the conclusion of a contractual agreement (e.g., LOI, SPA, valuation mandate) between Principal (investor, developer) and Agent (real estate broker, appraiser).

While the investors tend to be fully transparent with their appraisers, they still do not want to disclose all property information to the real estate brokers. In this sense, the main category of non-disclosed information to real estate brokers is related to the tenancy situation (agreements with tenants, lease income, other strategic information).

Further on, the real estate brokers' behavior is characterized by three main aspects in the relationship with the Principal after a contract is signed (in most cases LOI, in which the broker receives the mandate for the commercialization of a real estate property).

On one hand, their involvement in the transaction process becomes lower because they have the certitude of receiving the agreed fee after the conclusion of the transaction. They want to control the process on both buyer's and seller's sides, therefore preferring to act as dual agents. The brokers want to lower the target sale price in the negotiations with a potential buyer in order to raise the chances of a having a concrete transaction.

Lastly, after having signed a valuation mandate, the appraisers still illustrate information asymmetries that come from the client's (Principal's) side, such as lack of transparency in the provided information as well as asymmetric behavior due to the time pressure they exercise.

6 Conclusions

6.1. Results of the interviews and implications

6.1.1. *Behavioral Real Estate*

The target of the study was to identify behaviors underlying the construct of interest of the real estate market actors – clients as well as service providers. Part of the original motivation was also to formalize the ethics issue in business relationships between the market actors and investigate whether the real estate organizations with their ethics principles play a significant role for appraisers, real estate brokers, and investors.

First of all, the analysis presented in the previous chapters reveals that both categories of market actors (clients and service providers) illustrate similar motives to be part of a real estate organization. These motives can be structured as follows:

1. When acting in an international business environment, memberships are seen as beneficial. This fact is mostly argued by the market actors from Central and Eastern Europe, and less by those who are active on the Austrian real estate market.
2. The values represented by real estate organizations play a notable role for the market actors, business ethics, code of conduct, confidentiality, professionalism, and transparency being the most used terms.
3. Networking as well as information exchange between market actors.
4. Education and continuous career development.
5. The service providers aim to signalize their professional standard they want to represent.

To sum up, an international or institutional business environment, the values represented by real estate organizations, networking, continuous education, as well as signaling are the main motives of the real estate market actors to decide upon a membership in a real estate organization.

By contrast, considerations such as personal network, local business environment, no direct business advantage, financial aspects, and substitutes play a role for real estate brokers, appraisers, and investors who choose to not opt for a membership.

These motives can be summarized as follows:

1 The existence of a strong personal network in the real estate business environment.
2 Local business environment, no internationality.
3 No direct business advantage, no direct mandates or businesses undertaken due to memberships.
4 Financial aspects, membership costs.
5 Substitutes: international agencies instead of organizations.

The next part of the chapter revealed a deeper understanding of the advisors' perspectives related to the mandates received through real estate organizations. While the private network (mostly for real estate brokers) and the in-house valuation department (in the case of the appraisers working for larger agencies) are the main reasons why the service providers do not need to search for mandates through real estate associations, most of the advisors make use of such organizations in order to approach potential clients or even more (e.g., events, networking), to have an already-established network for the acquisition of new ones.

Broadly, this work also opens a rather underestimated research topic on the relationship between the brokerage, valuation, and investment departments of big agencies, and on how the mandates are commissioned by the clients coming from an international or an institutional business environment; how the so-called "Chinese walls" function, taking into account the competition between the service companies on the (international and/or institutional) real estate market; and the fact that the brokerage or valuation services are seemingly not always fully separated from the transaction process.

The second part of the study focuses on three main areas in Behavioral Real Estate: *valuation rationale*, with an attempt in explaining the interests of the market actors in commercial property valuation; *valuation anchoring* (also known as *availability heuristics*, *confirmation bias*), or how the appraisers tend to takeover assumptions from previous valuation reports, as well as *client feedback*, and the relationships between market actors; finally, the section closes with an enumeration of the generic value drivers of the real estate market actors.

The results of the research show that in order to explain the valuation rationale of the market actors, we need to take a deeper look into each party's interest, whether it is a real estate broker, an appraiser, an investor, or a developer of commercial property assets.

The results of the interviews show that brokers want to convince their clients about a certain value (as transaction price) and they are ready to refuse a mandate for the commercialization of a property if they consider the expectations of the clients differ from their own opinion. Moreover, this study questions the Chinese walls within big agencies, since evidence shows that the real estate brokers gather information from their in-house departments, such as valuation or investment.

In trying to explain the valuation rationale, the results of the present research exhibit that the appraisers consider valuation reports to be subjective, flexible, and might suffer value deviations of 10–15% as compared to an initial result. The main parameters that influence the outcome are *one-time valuations*, *yield*, *NOI*, *and comparable transactions*.

Furthermore, the real estate investors develop a common opinion that the value of the property needs to remain stable throughout the valuation process, and until the property is sold. Accordingly, when a property is in acquisition, the aim is that its value rises and becomes higher than the acquisition price. Finally, the investors explain that a property needs to be sold above its book value and they express the concern that when appraisers are changed, the property value suffers deviations.

The analysis and the outcomes presented also reveal that the results of the research are consistent with previous ones in the field of *valuation anchoring*. The main reason for that is the lack of experience with a certain asset class or real estate market. It is also interesting to note that the opinions of the appraisers claiming that their margin of flexibility for a certain valuation outcome becomes lower when previous valuation reports that have been made for the same property – under the same conditions – are available.

Furthermore, this study has also contributed to Behavioral Real Estate research, focusing on explaining the relationships between the market actors in property valuation for transaction purposes. The main evidence comes from the importance appraisers give to *client feedback*, and their aim to focus on long-term partnerships with their clients. When this is given, the degree of flexibility in valuation reports rises; otherwise, the advisors (appraisers, real estate brokers) conduct a client screening before entering into a contractual relationship. *Feedback is essential*, but there are also disclaimers – the research shows that the appraisers give high importance to the opinion of third parties (e.g., fiscal authorities, financial institutions).

Lastly, the aim of this research was to identify behaviors underlying the construct of interests (value drivers) of the real estate market players in commercial real estate valuation for transaction purpose.

The clients share similar views related to their focus (*book value*, *yield*, *valuation result*, *market environment*, *ethics of the business partner*) and concerns (*the non-transparency in the CEE real estate markets*, *the rent-free periods which are not always fully known by the appraisers*, *the dual function of the real estate broker*).

On the other hand, the service providers want *long-term relationships* with their clients and give the highest importance to the *contractual fee* they negotiate. *Data quality*, *timeframe*, *and marketability of the property* are further value drivers, especially for the real estate brokers, while appraisers concentrate on the *validity of the valuations towards third parties* (e.g., financial or fiscal institutions). The main concern of the real estate brokers lies in the *questionable business ethics in CEE*. On the other hand, the appraisers mention the *client's pressure* – either as time pressure or expectations on a certain valuation outcome.

To conclude, there is a large discrepancy between the normative valuation process (given by laws, norms, and regulations on a national and international level), and the actual process in commercial property valuation, which is subject to the interests of the involved market actors. The valuation outcome might be reduced to a confirmation given by the appraiser to the investor, while the real estate broker focuses on the fast marketability of the property.

6.1.2. Principal-Agent problem and moral hazard in real estate

The last part of this study aims to fill in the literature gap between Behavioral Real Estate and agency problems. Salzman and Zwinkels (2017: 99) also note this interrelation: "Availability heuristic, confirmation bias and anchoring help to explain the discrepancy to a high extend, whereas client pressure is shown to make appraisers revise their valuation due to agency problems."

Moreover, they point out that biases in valuations cannot be explained only by heuristics (Salzman & Zwinkels 2017: 91), but by additional insights on the asymmetric information between market actors.

Before entering a contractual agreement (either binding or non-binding), the real estate investors are generally cautious with the information they disclose and might even participate in certain transaction processes in order to gain market information, and not because of a real interest in a property acquisition. Specifically, the investors and developers communicate differently with the service providers.

On one hand, they might not want to disclose certain information to their appraisers, such as void periods, rent-free periods, capital expenditure, tenancy situation, and future acquisitions. Furthermore, they are cautious when working together with appraisers from large agencies and question the Chinese wall between departments such as valuation, brokerage, and investment.

By contrast, the real estate investors and developers show an even deeper lack of confidence in the relationship with the brokers. They argue that the information received is not fully accurate and explain that this causes the lack of trust towards brokers.

Valuation reports, information regarding the tenancy situation, project timeline, and capital expenditure are examples of information not disclosed to real estate brokers. Additionally, the investors tend to not trust those real estate brokers that act as dual agents and represent both parties (buyer and seller).

Before concluding a contract with the clients, the appraisers raise three main concerns: they need a concrete fee settlement, want to prepare a draft calculation in order to estimate whether they meet their clients' expectations, and they want to assess the work load for the valuation report they have to prepare. Here, the appraisers mention that the "uncomplicated" mandates are often favored.

The real estate brokers have the commercialization of the properties as main interest, mostly those "easily to be sold." In order to not hinder or delay an acquisition, the real estate brokers might choose not to disclose (full) information on the tenancy situation, balance sheets, turnover, neighboring buildings, information on early access for the properties under development, detailed technical specifications, or layouts. Yield compression might be also a strategy of large agencies in order to receive a mandate for brokerage services.

After entering a contractual agreement, the investors show a high degree of transparency towards their appraisers, whereas they might still choose not to disclose specific information – mainly related to the tenancy situation – to the real estate brokers involved.

The behavior of the real estate brokers after having signed a contract (LOI, NDA, etc.) is characterized by three main aspects. First, their involvement is lower since they have established a contact between buyer and seller and defined their fee; second, they prefer to act as dual agents in order to have control over the transaction process; third, the brokers might want to influence – and lower – the target sale price in order to have a concrete transaction, and thus receive the agreed brokerage fee.

Finally, the information asymmetries between clients and appraisers are still maintained after concluding a contract for the valuation mandate. The lack of information availability or transparency, as well as time pressure towards appraisers, are the two most important elements that could be identified in this study.

Based on the aforementioned evidence, we can sketch the forms of information asymmetries between the real estate market actors in commercial property valuation and real estate transactions:

Asymmetric information	***Forms***
Hidden characteristics	*Investors* avoid disclosing certain characteristics or information (NOI, rent free, CapEx, tenant information, valuation reports, project timeline) *Brokers* do yield compression or retain certain information on tenancy, early access, completion date or technical specifications, neighborhood situation
Hidden intentions	*Investors* participate at initial biddings in order to gain market information *Appraisers* assess the work load, the information availability, client's expectations, before signing the contract *Brokers* convince the investor (seller) about lowering the value, in order to conduct the transaction
Hidden action	*Brokers* do not follow the project in an active way after having signed an LOI; they may also want to only choose projects they consider easy to market; prefer the dual function in order to have control on the transaction; want to lower the target (asking) price of their clients in order to conduct a transaction; show the property in a more positive light, disregarding possible vacancy difficulties by mentioning the easy marketability
Hidden information	*Investors* do not want to disclose specific side agreements with tenants or strategic information, if not evidenced in the sale agreement documentation or other agreements with tenants *Appraisers* do not have enough information, documentation, or information transparency

Figure 6.1 Forms of information asymmetries in real estate valuation and transactions

6.2. Conclusions

This work provides a robust result in the area of Behavioral Real Estate Economics and consistent evidence for the Principal-Agent problem in commercial property valuation for transaction purposes.

On one hand, the research conducted demonstrates that the Agent (illustrated in this work as a real estate service provider, such as an appraiser or real estate broker) has his own personal objective to augment his benefits in a real estate transaction or valuation mandate, aiming to maximize his profit with the lowest effort possible.

On the other hand, the Principal (illustrated in this work as a real estate investor or developer) might not provide the expected quality of information, and from this arises a non-satisfactory valuation result delivered by the appraiser.

The null hypotheses in this work was that the Principal is not satisfied with the service delivered by the Agent, and this lack of trust is caused by the former's experience in real estate transactions and real estate valuations. This is the reason why the Principal wants to have the control over the Agent, and wants to cover the potential risks in a transaction or valuation through guarantees, non-disclosure clauses, and binding agreements.

This study, conducted through interviews with 52 real estate market actors, demonstrated that this hypothesis is true. Furthermore, the research also indicates that the Agents are not a neutral partner towards the other Principals, therefore there is a lack of mutual trust between the Principal and the Agent, which leads to asymmetric information on real estate markets. To conclude, the business relationship between the Principal and the Agent is asymmetric because of the lack of reliance between the real estate market actors.

To ensure robustness and fidelity of the final product, the work also contributes to the Behavioral Real Estate literature and adds new concepts and deeper explanations to the findings of James Graaskamp (1933–1988).

It is shown that the behavior of appraisers, brokers, and investors is led by the interests they have in a property valuation or transaction. This work contributes significantly to the empirical literature on Behavioral Real Estate research, with focus on valuation rationale, valuation anchoring, and client feedback. Moreover, the study includes an investigation of the value drivers of the real estate market actors, as well as their behavior towards real estate organizations, especially related to business ethics.

Finally, the evidence from this study leads to a deeper definition of the forms of information asymmetries between the market actors in commercial property valuation and transactions.

From the aforementioned results of the research, it can be derived that the valuation process for transaction purposes takes place under the influence of the *behavior* of the real estate market actors, determined by their interests, but also depending on third-party opinions (such as financing institutions, other appraisers, certain authorities).

Thus, provided the valuation norms, laws, or standards (either national or international) are respected, until reaching the final property value, the behavior of the real estate market actors plays a decisive role.

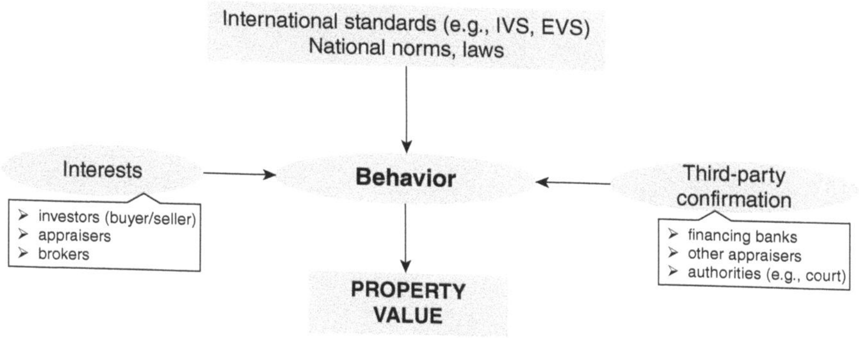

Figure 6.2 The behavioral framework of market actors

The aim of this study was to bring further evidence in the field of Behavioral Real Estate and develop the forms of information asymmetries in the Principal-Agent problem related to commercial property valuation for transaction purposes, with Austria and Central and Eastern Europe as focus markets. Furthermore, it is also aimed to motivate researchers and professionals to pursue deeper studies in this domain. Such research could generally help the real estate market actors recognize the behavioristic nature of their business and the interests of the other real estate market participants.

As Salzman and Zwinkels (2017: 100) note, "the importance of behavior embedded in the decision of intervening in the real estate market either as a consumer or investor is undeniable," thus future research in Behavioral Real Estate could also "induce policymakers to 'nudge' the real estate market towards more efficiency."

Overall, one of the main objectives should remain bridging the gap between professional, practice-based real estate and academic research.

Bibliography

Salzman, Diego & Zwinkels, Remco (2017): Behavioral Real Estate. *Journal of Real Estate Literature*. Vol. 25. No. 1

Annexes

Annex 1 NVivo – Classification sheet: Advisors

Nr.	*Participant code (incl. asset classes)*	*Principal / Agent*	*Expertise in Countries*	*Company size*	*Member*
1	ABLOR01	Agent	SI	small	no
2	ABL02	Agent	RO	large	no
3	ABVLOR03	Agent	AT	small	no
4	ABVLOR04	Agent	AT CZ HU SK RO SI	small	yes
5	ABR05	Agent	AT	small	no
6	ABLOR06	Agent	AT CZ HU SK SI	large	no
7	ABLOR07	Agent	AT CZ HU SK RO SI	large	no
8	AVOR08	Agent	AT	large	yes
9	AVLOR09	Agent	RO	large	yes
10	AVLOR10	Agent	AT CZ HU SK RO SI	large	yes
11	ABLOR11	Agent	RO	large	no
12	AVLOR12	Agent	AT	small	yes
13	ABLO13	Agent	RO	large	no
14	ABOR14	Agent	AT SK CZ	small	no
15	AVLOR15	Agent	RO	small	yes
16	ABLOR16	Agent	RO	large	no
17	AVLOR17	Agent	RO	large	yes
18	ABLOR18	Agent	RO	large	no
19	AVLOR19	Agent	HU	large	yes
20	ABVLOR20	Agent	AT	small	yes
21	ABLOR21	Agent	AT	medium	yes
22	ABVLOR22	Agent	AT RO	small	yes
23	AVLOR23	Agent	AT	small	yes
24	ABVLOR24	Agent	AT RO	medium	yes
25	ABLOR25	Agent	AT CZ SK SI RO HU	small	yes
26	AVLOR26	Agent	AT HU	small	yes
27	AVLOR27	Agent	AT	small	yes
28	AVLOR28	Agent	AT	small	yes

Annex 2 NVivo – Classification sheet: Clients

Nr.	*Participant code (incl. asset classes)*	*Principal / Agent*	*Expertise in Countries*	*Public company (current/ background)*	*Company size*	*Member*
1	PLOR01	Principal	RO HU	no	large	yes
2	PLOR02	Principal	CZ HU RO SI SK	no	medium	yes
3	PL03	Principal	RO	no	small	no
4	PL04	Principal	AT SK SI	no	small	yes
5	PLOR05	Principal	CZ HU RO SI SK	no	medium	yes
6	PL06	Principal	CZ HU SK	yes	large	yes
7	PLR07	Principal	AT SK SI	no	small	no
8	PLOR08	Principal	CZ HU RO SI SK	no	medium	no
9	PL09	Principal	AT	no	small	no
10	PLO10	Principal	AT	no	small	no
11	PR11	Principal	AT	no	large	yes
12	PLO12	Principal	AT HU RO SK	no	large	no
13	POR13	Principal	CZ SK SI	yes	large	no
14	PLOR14	Principal	AT CZ HU SK RO	yes	medium	yes
15	PLO15	Principal	AT CZ HU SK RO	yes	large	no
16	PLOR16	Principal	CZ HU SK SI RO	yes	large	no
17	PLOR17	Principal	AT CZ HU SK RO SI	no	small	yes
18	PLOR18	Principal	AT CZ HU SK RO SI	no	small	yes
19	POR19	Principal	AT HU	no	small	yes
20	PO20	Principal	AT HU	yes	large	no
21	PLOR21	Principal	AT SI	no	medium	no
22	PR22	Principal	AT CZ HU SK RO SI	no	medium	no
23	POR23	Principal	HU RO CZ	yes	large	no
24	PLOR24	Principal	AT CZ HU SK RO SI	no	small	no

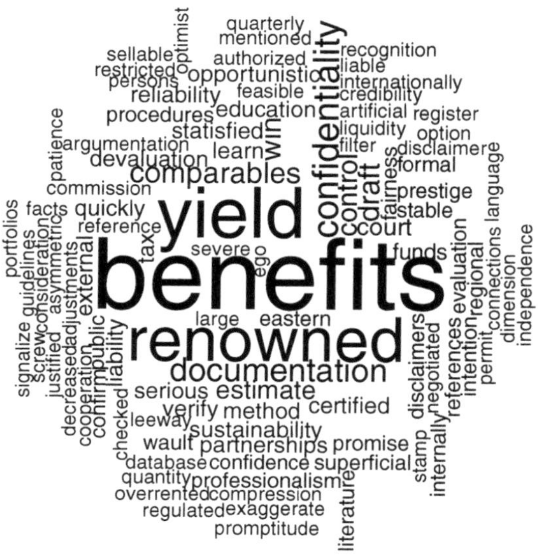

Annex 3 NVivo – Word Cloud of the entire project

Index

Note: Numbers in *italics* indicate figures on the corresponding page.

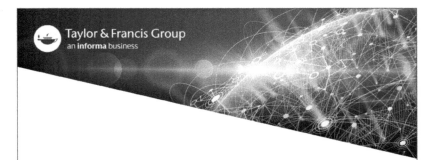

For Product Safety Concerns and Information please contact our EU
representative GPSR@taylorandfrancis.com
Taylor & Francis Verlag GmbH, Kaufingerstraße 24, 80331 München, Germany

www.ingramcontent.com/pod-product-compliance
Ingram Content Group UK Ltd.
Pitfield, Milton Keynes, MK11 3LW, UK
UKHW021848240425
457818UK00020B/768
* 9 7 8 0 3 6 7 5 1 7 5 9 5 *